LEADING GROUPS IN PERSONAL GROWTH

Jackie M. Smith

JOHN KNOX PRESS
Richmond, Virginia

Scripture is from The New English Bible, © The Delegates of the Oxford
University Press and the Syndics of the Cambridge University Press, 1961.

The excerpt by Carl R. Rogers is from *Conflict and Creativity,* edited by
Seymour M. Farber and R. H. L. Wilson. Copyright © 1963 by McGraw-
Hill, Inc. Used with permission of McGraw-Hill Book Company.

The excerpts by Rollo May are reprinted from *Love and Will* by Rollo
May. By permission of W. W. Norton & Company, Inc. Copyright © 1969
by W. W. Norton & Company, Inc.

International Standard Book Number: 0-8042-9015-6
© John Knox Press 1973
Printed in the United States of America

Contents

The Three Approaches for Using This Guide

This leader's guide created for use with the student's text *Face to Face* is primarily focused on experience-centered learning as one of the best means of freeing persons to grow toward maturity as children of God. Major space is given to this first approach, partly because of its great value, and partly because no other resource for leaders like it is known to exist. Exercises contained in Approach I can be useful in any personal growth or human development group.

However, as the Introduction makes clear, many leaders and groups are not ready for the kind of involvement that is required in such experience-centered learning. For them, two additional ways of using the text *Face to Face* are offered.

Approach II calls for using *Face to Face* as a basis for *Bible study,* with primary emphasis on the last three sections. Session-by-session help for such Bible study on the themes of these major chapters begins on page 161.

Approach III is through discussion of the *content* of *Face to Face,* and this approach too assumes that little or no use will be made of the exercises in Approach I. Helps for discussion are offered in "Suggestions for Thought and Action," found at the end of each chapter, and in discussion questions suggested on pages 173–178 in this volume.

To further enrich discussion or either of the other two approaches, a wide variety of films is recommended for each chapter, also in Approach III.

Approach I

EXPERIENCE-CENTERED LEARNING

Introduction

PURPOSE OF THIS STUDY EVENT

This study framework was created to provide learning *experiences* through which persons may (1) grow in awareness of their uniqueness as individual creatures created in the image of God for a divine purpose; (2) explore from a theological and psychological perspective their individual natures ("being simultaneously merely-creaturely and godlike, strong and weak, limited and unlimited, merely-animal and animal-transcending, adult and child, fearful and courageous, progressing and regressing, yearning for perfection and yet afraid of it, being a worm and also hero"[1]); (3) explore from a psychological and theological perspective their communal nature—their need for community and for a deeper level of communication with other people and with God; (4) gain insight into and skills for deeper levels of communication and greater self-awareness; and (5) discover how these skills and insights can be used in continued growth toward authentic, healthy selfhood, so that each person is moving toward becoming the person he was created to be and deeply needs to become.

The key phrase in the purpose stated above is *to provide learning experiences.* The entire study is structured for *experience-centered learning,* for event, for happening.

This means the study is NOT created to—
1) have a teacher in the traditional sense;
2) have student-listeners;
3) provide a description of what a mature person *should be,* so that a person can then try to become like that picture;
4) simply increase intellectual information *about* how persons become more mature;
5) provide a traditional study-learning event.

The study *is created to—*
1) have learner-teacher-leaders;
2) have additional learner-teacher-participants;
3) allow participants to provide their own course content;
4) use the participant's book as information for reflecting upon and gaining insight into group and individual experiences;
5) use selected exercises from which group experiences emerge to become the course content;
6) provide opportunity for personal change and growth.

Assumptions Behind This Study Event

It is assumed that class participants have a foundational knowledge of the Christian faith and that they are seeking to find ways to grow as persons committed to the life and destiny of mankind revealed in Jesus Christ.

Why Experience-Centered Learning?

The goal of experience-centered learning is to effect *awareness and change*—awareness of personal life-style and change (growth) in life-style when a person desires change. This means the goal of learning events is continued *conversion*. Conversion into the Christian faith is not just a one-time thing. It is an ongoing process as people grow and mature. Such conversional growth does not occur simply by acquiring more or deeper intellectual knowledge of the faith, dogmas, moral codes, and statements of belief. Instead, Christ reveals a life-giving quality that continues to change all of life, affecting values, attitudes, actions, life-styles, and human relationships. All belief about Christ remains unreal and external until it is rooted in and validated by human experience. In other words, the Christian life must be lived. Therefore, this study has been created to—

1) help people become more aware of the life-style they have already developed through significant relationships, religious and cultural influences, self-determination, etc.; and

2) help people discover options available to them for further self-directed growth as they seek to live out their faith.

How Life-Changing Growth Occurs

R. D. Laing has said, "We do not need theories so much as the experience that is the source of the theory." This is true because intellectual understanding alone does not of itself bring growth. In addition, it has been estimated that persons remember 10 percent of what they hear, 30 percent of what they see, 50 percent of what they both see and hear, and 90 percent of what they do; consequently, a course seeking to provide an opportunity for personal growth must place heavy emphasis on participation, involvement, action, analysis, decision-making (about changes one desires), and experimentation (putting into practice new behavior decided upon). Although cognitive learning will take place, the focus is on the affective domain—feelings, needs, values, attitudes, and relationships.

The basic flow of experience-centered learning is:

1) Experience—DO
2) Explore experience—LOOK
3) Analyze experience—REFLECT, DISCOVER
4) React—RESPOND
5) Determine—DECIDE
6) Experiment—LEARN, GROW

Let us look more carefully at each phase of experience-based learning.

1) *Experience.* A situation will be created to involve participants. An experience will flow from the situation. In this experience participants will react in their "normal" manner. For example: One day in an eleventh-grade class, a teacher desiring to involve students in a study of the effect of rapid change upon people created radical changes in the normal class procedures. Operating under the new regime for a fifteen-minute period, the students were able to actually experience people's reaction to change. It is interesting to note that in the thirty minutes of discussion which followed, the class reported from their own experience every reaction to change generally listed in psychology books (and a few new ones!).

It is important to remember that in experience-centered learning *no* situation can fail to provide an opportunity for learning. No exercise can fail! Regardless of what happens in the exercise, participants have had a common experience to which they can react. Even though situation exercises provided in this course were created for a particular purpose, there are no *correct* reactions. Every reaction is valid; consequently, a group can learn from anything which occurs. This is true even if the reaction is "I felt that was a stupid thing to do and I felt silly and embarrassed." No opportunity for learning needs to be lost if the group examines immediate reactions to what actually occurred in the common experience. Once honest feelings and responses have been shared, questions such as the following will allow persons to learn from a common experience—even one which may have appeared stupid to some: What made you think it was stupid? What made you feel silly or embarrassed? What prevented you from really entering into the exercise? In other words, from the common experience, move on to the next step and examine the experience which *actually took place* and the learnings which are possible from it.

The only two factors which can cause an exercise to fail are (1) the leader's determination to see that a particular response occurs or that a particular truth should be learned from the experience; or (2) the unwillingness of the participants to share their real reactions and feelings.

2) *Explore.* Since we do not automatically learn from experience, it is necessary to look at the experience to see what happened.

Ways we "see" are:

a) Sharing the data of the experience (anything all participants saw and heard).

b) Observing participants' own feelings and reactions during their participation in the exercise; whatever their feelings, they are important.

c) Sharing individual feelings and reactions to the event.

d) Communicating how individuals or the group affected particular persons during the exercise. This kind of "feedback" communication should be given as soon after the behavior referred to as possible. (See pages 123–124 for a fuller statement about feedback.)

e) Responding to feedback, if individuals given feedback desire to respond. Feedback should not be argued about, since it is a statement of how one person experienced something. Each communication should be accepted as an honest statement of what the speaker felt. The one who is given feedback is left free to accept or reject it.

3) *Analyze.* Next the group analyzes various aspects of the experience. They discover and reflect on what was really happening. What parts of the experience affected us most? In what ways did it affect us? Why did some of us react to the same action differently? What did the experience show us about ourselves? our feelings? our responses? the way we affect others? What in us caused that effect? What does this tell us about the way we interact with these people? Of course, these questions should be geared to the specific experience.

4) *React.* Only the individual can decide how he will respond to what has happened, but it is helpful to explore this area with the group. Questions such as these are appropriate: What new insights did I gain about myself? about others? about human interaction in general? about life? What difference will it make in my life? What will I do differently next time? What will I do in the same manner? What do I want to work on? What do I want to check out with others? What do I like about the way I acted? What strengths does that action show? (Additional questions may be asked, based on the shared events.) It helps for individuals to verbalize their learnings and to check them out with others, *if* they so desire.

5) *Determine.* If the individual has grown in awareness of self and others, growth has occurred. He is changed, for his world is bigger, and he can act with new awareness. Now the individual can make wiser decisions about directions for self-growth. Only the individual can decide what he will do with what he has experienced, but supportive and nurturing group life can provide a seedbed that encourages individuals to make realistic decisions on the basis of greater awareness now available to them.

6) *Experiment.* The supportive group will encourage and allow participants to try out new ways of perceiving, thinking, relating, and responding within the group situation. Unless a person is

given an opportunity to try out new behavior, his learnings may soon die. Relevant change is difficult unless a person can make experimental efforts in a relatively safe and supportive situation.

A Different Sort of Learning

Obviously, we are describing a kind of teaching-learning situation that may be new to many people. And, as you know, there is often considerable resistance to the new. What do we have going for us which may overcome or minimize this resistance? There are at least four basic points of "reality contact" which, if seen, may free a group to step outside the security of the familiar cognitive methods of learning and risk experience-based growth learning.

1) *Need.* All human beings feel the need for change and growth. Some may be less aware of that need for others, but the need is a part of human life.

2) *Failure.* At some point in life, each of us has experienced the inadequacy of just intellectual knowledge about a better way of life to bring about desired life changes. Paul expressed a universal experience of men as he said, "For the good that I would I do not: but the evil which I would not, that I do." (Rom. 7:19, K.J.V.) Every person has experienced the thrill of being motivated by some stimulating sermon, lesson, or book to commit himself to change ("When I get home, I'm going to act differently!"), only to find that when he does get home the newly acquired insight is quickly overwhelmed or forgotten in the maze of old habits, attitudes, threats, and tensions.

3) *Success.* Psychological research indicates that when individuals allow themselves to become more aware of deeper levels of themselves, as they grow in self-knowledge, they are freed to reorganize their lives and relationships in ways they desire, in ways they see as being more natural, constructive, and satisfying. In other words, it is not just intellectual understanding of how I

ought to act that brings change. Instead, it is self-knowledge that frees one for change. Self-knowledge puts one in touch with his basic drive toward self-actualization and maturity. As this drive is unleashed, intellectual knowledge of desired ethical behavior may be of help as the person gets in touch with his own growth process. Although we have all experienced some level of this kind of basic change within ourselves, many of us are not aware of exactly how it happened.

4) *Truth validates itself.* As people grow in awareness of self and others, and experience growth within their persons, they will become convinced of the validity of the process that frees them to grow.

Can we simply ask people who are not familiar with experienced-based learning to risk something new? Curiosity is a strong motivating factor, and throughout the ages man has been curious about his enigmatic nature. Dare we challenge people to use their curiosity in a new venture that may free them to move toward fuller growth in their journey toward maturity in Christ (Col. 1:28)?

THE EDUCATIONAL CLIMATE
AND THE ROLE OF THE LEADER

These two aspects of the educative-growth process will be described together since climate is a result of human interaction. This interaction you will initiate. This means you are an important resource for this course. Your most important function as a leader is the development of a facilitating, helping climate. Let us look at the characteristics of this kind of climate.

Trust in the human being (yourself as well) as one who can develop his God-given potentials is a basic, necessary element in the kind of growth situation we have been describing. Unless you can initiate an atmosphere in which basic trust can be developed, others will be unable to risk gaining deeper knowledge of themselves. Can you accept the truth that God created each person to become free? Can you trust others to exercise that freedom without feeling the need to tell them what they ought to think, do, become?

A second necessary element is *acceptance*. If persons are to delve into deeper levels of self-understanding, they must know that they are valued and that their attitudes, feelings, fears, joys, will be respected. Can you accept people as they now are, imperfect sinners loved by God, struggling sinners longing for fuller life? In an atmosphere of trusting acceptance, persons can more nearly accept themselves, learn more about themselves, and move toward fuller exercise of their freedom for self-directed change.

A third necessary element is *deep, empathetic understanding*. Can you listen to others in such a way that you begin to feel and understand the other person's feelings and actions as he does? Will you be able to understand from the participant's viewpoint what is going on inside him as he tells you, or will you be reading your own feelings and thoughts and judgments into what he says?

If you come up with a number of negative answers to the questions above, and if you can admit that to others, and if you want to do something about them, then I suspect you are the right person to be a leader in such a study. Of course all "yeses" would be great! But in reality probably all of us need to grow in trust, in accepting love, in empathetic understanding. If we are willing to admit this need, to recognize and acknowledge that we too will be learners in this class, then we are ready to begin. The most important resource you have to bring to this learning situation is your real self. As nearly as possible, (1) *be who you are* without facades or masks; (2) *show who you are* without fear of your feelings, your inadequacies, or your strengths; and (3) *trust your humanness* to call forth greater humanness in others.

Additional resources you have are (1) the experience-centered learning exercises (pp. 30–118), and (2) materials included in Approaches II and III (pp. 161–178). The experience-creating exercises are the backbone of this study. They are tools for engaging in group experience from which participants create their own study content. It is important to remember that in relation to these exercises, a part of your function is to have materials for exercises available as needed. Also, any special knowledge or experience you have should always be available to participants, but it should never be imposed on them. Materials in Approaches II and III provide possibilities for information-centered learning sessions which may be called for occasionally in your work together. Remember that your basic resource is the group of persons who are gathered for continued growth.

ROLE OF THE PARTICIPANTS

Members of your class who have had no opportunity for experience-based learning may feel an initial frustration with a free sort of learning situation in which the class creates the basic material from which they learn. However, experience indicates that if the leader is secure enough to bear this initial frustration, the frustration is transformed into creative energy as participants become more involved in group activity.

You will be dealing with questions (Who am I? How can I become what I deeply long to be?) that are vital concerns of all people. As members of your class begin to realize that through their involvement with others they are really growing in understanding of themselves and others, they will be willing to invest more and more of themselves in the learning process. Self-investment is the major ingredient needed from each group member. If members are willing to risk sensitive engagement in whatever is going on, even if it at first appears to be a gimmick, you as a group leader will have little to worry about.

It should be made clear from the beginning that learning and teaching are group tasks. The class should know that the traditional role of the teacher (one who gives and interprets information) will not be filled in the conventional sense. Each participant should understand that as individuals share their feelings, attitudes, and perceptions about others and the experience, group members will learn from each other. In this sense everyone becomes a teacher. And as participants listen carefully to each other, everyone becomes a learner.

Ground Rules for the Class

It may be helpful at the initiation of this study of personal growth to indicate as briefly as possible the central points of experience-centered learning. Decide whether you think this is necessary or not. If some introductory statement seems needed, simply explain anything that will be new and different about the time you spend together.

Members of your class may be familiar with discovery learning or inductive learning, in which persons draw conclusions from the learning experience itself. These methods differ from the more familiar deductive method of learning, in which one acquires intellectual content and then moves to specific application of the content. Experience-centered learning is based upon the inductive approach, but it moves beyond the usual inductive method since it does not view *discussion* of truths discovered as the end product. Instead, it moves on to decision-making and experimentation. Group members learn primarily from the experience they have as a group, reflecting upon what has happened as members act and react to one another, and as they free each other for actual experimentation with new patterns of thought and behavior. Learning defined as self-directed growth is the goal of this time together. Until what has been discovered and discussed has actually affected participants personally, the goal has not been reached.

However, it should be stressed that although the course is designed for personal growth—growth in self-awareness and self-disclosure—persons within the group should always be free. The following rules should be made clear and class members should be committed to them:

1) Any person is free *not* to participate in any activity.
2) No person should ever ask information of another which he is unwilling to give about himself.

It should also be made clear that the course is designed for personal growth, *not* group therapy. The course focuses on understanding and learning from one another, not on analyzing one another. If, during the time together, someone appears to be trying to analyze why a person behaves in a certain manner, it might be helpful to remind the group that the study is only concerned with the here and now, the immediacy of what is *present* and how the present is affecting persons and the group. The present experience can be dealt with in terms of learning how to understand and relate helpfully with persons within the group. (See the theory paper on page 130). As individuals grow in and through these relationships, they will be able to apply their learnings to "back home" relationships, for, indeed, they will be changed persons—persons who have been engaged in real learning.

An example of what can be expected is given in the report of a participant in a similar sort of learning situation:

In the course of this process, I saw hard, inflexible, dogmatic persons, in the brief period of several weeks, change in front of my eyes and become *sympathetic, understanding* and to a marked degree *non-judgmental.* I saw neurotic, compulsive persons ease up and become more accepting of themselves and others. In one instance, a student who particularly impressed me by his change, told me when I mentioned this: "It is true. I feel less rigid, more open to the world. And I like myself better for it. I don't believe I ever learned so much anywhere." I saw shy persons become less shy and aggressive persons more sensitive and moderate.

A more personal statement of this kind of change is given by a student at the end of the course.

Your way of being with us is a revelation to me. In your class I feel important, mature and capable of doing things on my own. I want to think for myself and this need cannot be accomplished through text books and lectures alone, but through living. I think you see me as a person with real feelings and needs, an individual. What I say and do are significant expressions from me, and you recognize this. . . . Eating an orange last week, I peeled the skin off each separate orange section and liked it better with the transparent shell off. It was juicier and fresher tasting that way. I began to think, that's how I feel sometimes, without a transparent wall around me, really communicating my feelings. I feel that I'm growing, how much, I don't know. I'm thinking, considering, pondering and learning.

. . . It is also clear that the student is closer to his own feelings, trusts them more, trusts himself more. He is not so afraid of his own spontaneity, not so afraid of change. He is, in short, learning what it means to be free.[2]

Changes can be expected from a learning process in which the emotional climate is warm, open, accepting, trusting, supportive, non-judgmental, and freeing. When individuals are respected and valued, they are freed to experience and share their feelings, emotions, and thoughts honestly and openly. When persons give full attention to the here and now as keen listeners, observers, and participants, they become mutual supporters for individual growth. They create an atmosphere of aliveness in which people discover that the core of real life is "to be caring"—to be "sensitively engaged in what's happening. Not *cautious* about life, but interested in *nurturing* life." [3]

Perhaps after these glowing words about what can happen, a word of warning may be in order. Do not expect, or lead participants to expect, an instant cure-all. Becoming a full human being is a lifetime process which is often accomplished through real struggle and pain. Growth which can occur within the supportive climate of your group should be viewed as strong medicine *strengthening* the self for fuller being and becoming. It is not, however, a miracle drug which, presto, produces totally new people.

To the degree that you feel it will be helpful to share this information about ground rules with the class participants, do so, but remember that *telling* won't accomplish the task. You may also want to share how you see your role as leader in this process, but your acts will speak louder than your words. As group leader, you are responsible for acts which initiate, encourage, enable, and help group members to build an open-caring life of their own. If you feel that telling what kind of atmosphere you are seeking to initiate would threaten participants (become an "ought" which would hinder free and open interchange), simply begin and see what happens. In either case, trust the Holy Spirit to be alive in you and the class as together you search for growth as children of God within his family.

USE OF THE PARTICIPANT'S BOOK

The participant's book, *Face to Face,* provides a conceptual or intellectual framework for understanding the self, others, relationships, communication, and the dynamics of human growth toward man's destiny. It was compiled to:

1) Give intellectual content that will help participants interpret what is actually happening in the class experience in the light of psychological, theological, and Biblical concepts. Since intellectual theory is most effective as it interprets something that has been recently experienced, assignments for reading about a particular area should follow as exercises related to that area.

2) Provide input for class discussions.

3) Provide a framework for the individual's understanding, growth, and development. You may want to stress the importance of individual work. The individual will benefit from this study in direct relationship to the degree of his own self-investment. This will also be true for you as a leader.

NUMBER OF LEADERS AND PARTICIPANTS

It is suggested that two leaders be selected for every ten to fifteen participants. Ideally, no class should be larger than fifteen members. If this study is used within the church school and classes are larger than fifteen members, consider breaking them into smaller units. If this is not possible, it will be necessary to divide the group into groups of fifteen or fewer for the exercises and reflection-action related to the exercises. This study may be most successful in newly created groupings with no past history of life together. However, if the group has been meeting together for some time, study with the group the theory paper on page 125.

Because of the kind of people-building, group-building venture you will be engaged in, it is imperative that group leaders *plan together* and work as co-leaders with equal responsibility for facilitating group life.

LEADER PREPARATION

Leaders should have had some prior experience in group dynamics, inductive learning experiences, or human relations labs. This would seem essential even if you use few exercises and concentrate on studying the concepts and Biblical passages in the student's book. Without the prior experience just referred to, it will be hard to grasp the full significance of the material and its potential influence on those who will open themselves to it.

Study

Preparation for this study should begin at least a month or two before initiation of the course. It should begin with a full individual study of this book and the participant's book. After such study, leaders will be ready to think together about their life with the class.

Objectives

A first step to focus your work is to state your objectives for the study—what do you want to happen to your class members as a result of this course, which is fundamentally concerned with personal growth and change? Answering the following question in specific detail will allow you to create objectives by which you can test whether you are accomplishing your task as you proceed: In what ways are people to be different as a consequence of this course?

The objectives listed below were in the mind of the writer as this study was put together. You will want to create your own objectives, in terms of your person and your group.

Each participant will show through his interaction in the group that he—

1) has gained new and deeper awareness of and insight into himself, his impact on others, and at least one other participant;

2) has improved or gained at least two skills for communication with others: listening skills, observing skills, skills in self-awareness and disclosure, and skills in communication;

3) has gained a better understanding of human interaction and interdependence.

In addition, each person will be able to talk about—

1) his understanding of the dynamics of human growth and change;

2) some growth that has occurred within him;

3) some previously unfulfilled potential or capacity that has been recognized and used;

4) some weakness or fear or anxiety that he would like to transform into creative energy;

5) some defense he would like to let go of;

6) a decision he has made about growth that he would like to nurture in himself and an awareness of aspects of his self that can be utilized for such growth;

7) a deeper desire for and understanding of how he can become more fully the person God created him to be.

These may sound like impossible objectives. Experience tells me that they are not. Within a nurturing climate, the Holy Spirit unleashed within persons is able to accomplish the impossible!

Movement

Throughout this study you will have to choose your own direction for movement of group life. This means *you* are really the creator of the study experience. Plans for each session include a number of exercises from which you can choose. In addition to these session plans and their exercises for experience-centered learning, there is material for two additional approaches or types of learning experiences: Bible study (Approach II, p. 161) and discussion of the text (Approach III, p. 171). You will probably want and need to intersperse some of these sessions with those which are experience-centered. But you alone can determine when they are needed.

Discussion of the text may be necessary from time to time if participants appear to have difficulty in understanding or applying what they have read to what is actually occurring in class. The best approach to this type of study is to encourage participants to indicate this need. At your first meeting, tell the class that this study is not planned to cover the content of the book; consequently, they are responsible for informing you of any need for exploration of book content. If they know this in advance, they can mark any passages they would like to discuss. You might suggest the following marking procedure if you think it will help class members take their responsibility seriously:

? "I don't believe that and I'd like to check it out with others."

! "That really makes sense and I'd like to tell others why."

+ "Maybe someone else can clarify or give me more information about this."

In addition, as the class explores the results of exercises, be aware of comments that may indicate a need for discussion sessions. If you or class members find such a need, the material in Approach III may be of help to you in planning your next meeting. In this section, a number of audio-visuals are suggested as triggers for discussion of each area of study. These films do not give answers. They are simply tools for stimulating thought. In addition, possible questions about the book content are also listed. These questions may help you direct discussion, but remember that rehashing information participants don't see the need of is relatively fruitless.

Bible study may be needed from time to time in order to relate Biblical concepts to what is occurring in actual experience. The sessions suggested in Approach II are related to Biblical studies listed in the "Suggestions for Thought and Action" sections of the student's book. Again, you and the participants will need to be alert to any need for further theological interpretation. A group with a deep understanding of the Christian faith may find no need for additional Bible study. A less firmly grounded group may find such study extremely beneficial. Ask group members to inform you if they have difficulty with the suggested Bible study itself or with its relationship to the other content in the student's book or to the group experience.

Yet another supplement to the experience-centered sessions would be the holding of *theory sessions* built around a paper in the resource section that is relevant to the interaction going on in your group. Such sessions should be used only after some group life has occurred through use of exercises, and should be followed by group experiences. They should be chosen according to the real needs of the group.

In a theory session, make the content of the paper your own and present it in lecture form, elaborating as necessary. Then hand out in duplicated form the information presented and have informal discussion of the material. (NOTE: The last two theory papers are copyrighted material from another source. You cannot duplicate them without permission of the publisher indicated on the first page of each.) Questions such as the following related to the specific paper might be helpful: Where have we experienced this happening among us? Has it been helpful or harmful in our group life? How could _____ (What? Be specific) help us as we create our life together? What will be necessary if we are to operate in _____ (such and such a manner)? You will need to think through specific questions related to each paper and your group experience before theory sessions. Avoid questions which can be answered with yes or no; such questions tend to cut off real thought and discussion. Also be careful in "why" questions not to threaten persons or to put them on the defensive. Instead of saying "Why did you do thus and so?" strive simply to explore what has been taking place, how people feel about it, what it means for your life together.

Remember that theory sessions should not replace group experience. If used, their purpose is (1) to help persons be more aware of the meaning of what *has* happened; (2) to be used in the future as helpful input to be reflected primarily in action.

Getting Organized

It is probably time to face the question, How on earth can you find your way through this mass of material?

1) Begin by familiarizing yourself with the various kinds of material available. Then you will be able to refer to it when the need or interest arises.

2) Remember that the basic purpose of the study is to learn from experiences. Consequently, your basic planning each week should start by reading the purpose of each session. Then, as you think through the exercises that follow, determine which exercise or exercises offer the best possibility for allowing your group to

accomplish that purpose. In making this choice you need to consider the following factors:

    a) your objectives for the study;

    b) the nature of the group—individual abilities, needs, fears, and interest, and, in groups which have met together prior to this study, previous group interaction;

    c) your own abilities, needs, desires, strengths, weaknesses;

    d) physical surroundings.

If you have had one meeting together, you will need to consider these additional elements:

    What has actually happened in your group life?

    —the freedom, openness, warmth which exist within the group—which sources of strength did you observe? How can you build on that? What is needed in group interaction? What is now possible for meeting this need?

    —the needs, desires, areas of heavy interest indicated in group interaction—what does this suggest about where you should move next?

Of course, as you consider these elements you may decide that another type of learning is called for. If so, turn to the other approaches and decide which.

3) As you move through this study do *not* feel constrained to "finish" one session in one class meeting. Your group might benefit by taking part in several exercises from the same session. It is far better to concentrate on meeting the needs of individuals and the group than to move slavishly through the sessions using one exercise from each session.

4) After the introductory session or sessions, you do not necessarily need to move through the sessions in the order printed. Let the group mold your movement. The sessions are related to the concerns of the pupil's book in the following manner:

    Sessions 2, 3, 4—"Loneliness—Love—Communication"

    Sessions 5, 6, 7—"Anxiety—Courage—Actualization"

Sessions 8, 9, 10, 11—"Emptiness—Integration—Valuing"
Session 12—concluding, summarizing session.

Since sessions 2–4 deal with basic communication skills, you may want to move through this section before others. However, if your group already communicates fairly easily at an open, depth level, you may want to move from session 1 to another section. Do not feel that you need to cover every session; omit or return to any session as group needs indicate. Feel free to adapt or change any exercise as work with your group indicates or dictates.

5) To do this kind of tailor-made course creation, it will be important to plan for the next meeting of the group as soon after the preceding one as possible. If you and your co-leader cannot meet immediately after the class session, jot down your immediate reactions, feelings, and thoughts about unmet needs observed, what you felt really happened, what that indicated about where you should move next, etc. Ask yourself what you learned, how you operated, what your feelings are about your role in the group. This material can act as a stimulus for further planning as you meet with your co-worker to make specific plans for the next session.

Setting

After you have determined your own objectives, move on to decide what kind of setting will be best for achieving them.

Due to the nature of this study, it would be extremely beneficial if the study could begin with a two-day, preferably, or one-day retreat in pleasant, restful, freeing physical surroundings; in fact, this study could be easily adapted for a week-long event which might have more far-reaching results in human growth and development than a year of hour-long sessions. An opening retreat setting would bring freedom from ordinary pressures and responsibilities, and give time and energy for the group's basic work of community building. Before you say, "But that's not possible here!" explore the possibility with group members and church officers and staff.

If in reality an opening retreat *is* impossible, consider an initial four-hour event which could create a core experience and impetus for further work together—perhaps a Saturday or Sunday afternoon, or an early supper followed by four hours of intensive work together.

Time Structure

After deciding upon the experience initiation, consider possible times for the remainder of the study. Is it possible for you to have more than one 1-to-1½-hour period a week? If so, you could accomplish even more. If not, this group work can be done within the 1-to-1½-hour framework, but in some instances it will be necessary to carry over the activities related to exploring the shared experience from one week to the next. This is not impossible, but it may be less effective, since an experience is best explored immediately after it has taken place.

Before you decide, consider the following:

1) Could you meet for twelve weeks in the afternoon or evening instead of on Sunday morning? If so, a 2-to-2½-hour session would be possible. Each exercise and follow-through could be more meaningful (life-changing) in a session of this length.

2) Could you use the regular church school hour as a time for discussion sessions? These could flow from questions which may have arisen as persons have dialogued with the participant's book or material suggested in the resource section or in the other approaches. Then your group could have lunch after the worship service and meet for a 2-to-2½-hour session for the exercise and follow-through activities. This would be extremely helpful, since you want the group work following each exercise to focus primarily on the content of the group experience and not simply on intellectual understandings.

3) Or could Sunday morning be used for information discussion and another 1½-to-2½-hour period be found during the week for the exercises? Don't say it is impossible—when people get turned on, there are possibilities. I once met for a year with a similar group from six to eight every Monday morning—rain, ice, or snow!

4) You and your class may think of additional possibilities to meet your needs, desires, and expectations.

Session

1

Purpose: To enable each person to present himself to the entire group and to hear others present themselves.

General Instructions

In this section (session 1) you will find a number of exercises to initiate a group experience in interpersonal relationships. This experience will be the content to be explored by your group. Note that some exercises are especially for newly formed groups. Others are more suitable for groups with a past history. If your group is composed of people who do not know each other, have large name tags available and ask each member to write the name he/she prefers to be called by.

You will also note that, throughout the session plans, a few exercises are labeled "high risk." These exercises are ones which are likely to involve participants in more intimate levels of self-revelation and group interaction. You and your co-leader will need to decide whether such exercises should be used in your group. In addition to considering whether your group desires or is ready for such experiences, decide whether you can deal with criticism or, more important, with the possible personal or interpersonal problems which might result from use of the exercises. A few exercises involve physical contact, which is often difficult for Americans. Others could generate more personal and interpersonal data than could be dealt with in a short period of time. You will need to think through each exercise and then make the decision on what is an appropriate learning opportunity for your group.

Room Arrangement

A must for this study is as informal and comfortable an atmosphere as possible. Both informality and comfort contribute to feelings of ease, human warmth, and openness. Chairs should be arranged so that all participants can see each other face to face. Perhaps a circular arrangement is best. Leaders should have no special place but should simply sit within the group. A lounge-type atmosphere is helpful. If there are tables in the room, you will need to remove them or arrange them in a circular or square fashion. If you will not be sitting around a table, suggest that persons bring a notebook or something hard to write upon.

Participant's Books

It would be good if books could be distributed at least two weeks before the first meeting. If this is possible, ask participants to read through chapter 2 before the first meeting.

If books cannot be distributed before the first meeting, you might consider using one or two of the films suggested for the introductory sessions in Approach III, page 172, and then have an exercise from those that follow in this section at your second meeting. Or you could go ahead with an exercise from this section, and hand out books about five minutes before the end of the session, asking participants to read through chapter 3 before the next meeting. Another possibility would be to distribute the books during the first session and to ask persons to read the first section, "So God Created Man," silently. Then, in the last fifteen to twenty minutes, ask each person to relate what he has read to his own life and share (1) what feelings he has about what has been read, and (2) what expectations he has for the remainder of the course. Ask all members to listen attentively to what is being said, for this is the beginning of your group-life experience. You and your co-leader should be aware of any shared information which might add to or alter your objectives. This alternative has the disadvantage of not allowing a great deal of time for personal interaction, which is to be your central focus, but it would help you to weave group members' expectations into your objectives.

If you are lucky enough to have a retreat or an extended first session, or if more time is available through a different schedule, you will be able to use a number of these exercises. This will give opportunity for your group to move to deeper and deeper levels of awareness of themselves, of others, and of group interaction. This will enhance the quality of your entire life together.

In addition to selecting and using a number of the exercises which follow in sessions 1 and 2, you might like to select a few from "Expressive Behavior," page 140. In a retreat setting you could also incorporate (according to needs you see) one or two theory and/or discussion sessions. The following papers from the resource section might be considered for an opening retreat: "Patterns of Interpersonal Relationship," page 125; "The Helping Relationship and Feedback," page 120; and "Awareness and Sensitivity in Interpersonal Relations," page 135.

However, in planning for a retreat a relaxed schedule is important. Plan for free time for informal conversation, rest, and play (organized and unorganized). These experiences can be as meaningful as structured group interaction. You might want to schedule some time for study of the participant's book and for group worship.

Your primary concern will be (1) to help provide a setting and atmosphere which is warm, accepting, and open; and (2) to think through a flow or movement of activities—ordering exercises for a variety of experiences and according to the level of involvement each requires. This will probably call for on-the-spot planning, in addition to prior planning. Move in the direction of deeper and deeper levels of self-investment and group involvement.

EXERCISES

Read the exercises carefully, selecting the one or two which you feel will best accomplish your objectives.

If your group is newly formed and members do not know each other well, the following exercise would be appropriate.

EXERCISE I. Get-Acquainted Questions

Purpose: To discover better ways of coming to know a (relative) stranger than the usual questions of "Where do you come from?" etc.

Directions:

Give your group the following instructions.

1) If you could ask just one question of each of the other members of your group, what would you ask that they would now be willing to answer frankly, and that would add most to your understanding of each of them as real persons? Think quietly, and write your questions down. Perhaps you will have several ideas, and you will want to write them all down before choosing your one best question.

2) Pair with a partner. Each of you is now to ask your question and to try your best to answer the question the other person will ask you.

3) Report to the group your question and how much you learned from it about your partner. Listen to all the others. See what questions proved most productive.

4) Review in your mind the various get-acquainted questions, and choose or invent the one you want to use the next time you are meeting someone new or any time you would like to avoid mere "cocktail-type" conversation.

5) If time permits, let each person pair off with another partner, and ask and answer the new questions.

6) In the group, let each report on how the questions worked this time.[1]

The following exercises could be used with new or old groups.

EXERCISE II. Deepening Mutual Understanding During
              Conversation

Purpose: 1) To develop skill in carrying forward a spontaneous
             conversation which brings a deepening understanding.
          2) To grow in ability to learn from others different from
             us.

Directions:

1) Who in this group seems *most like* yourself? In what way?
Let everyone answer.

2) Whom, in this group, do you see as *most different* from you?
In what way? Let everyone answer.

3) Select a pair who see themselves as quite similar. Try to
select two persons who seem fairly free, or ask for volunteers. Ask
them simply to begin a conversation in which they allow the interaction to flow along smoothly, but gradually move toward sharing
more that is personal and intimate. Other members of the group
observe quietly. If either of the active conversationalists wishes,
he may turn to one or more of the observers for advice and suggestions. Continue for ten minutes.

4) The observers then review the conversation. What thoughts
and feelings did they have as the talk progressed?

5) Now select, from among those who have been observers,
two people—this time on the basis of maximizing differences—so
that each of the original pair is paired with someone *unlike* himself. Divide the remainder of the class into two groups of ob-

servers, each to observe one of the new pairs. Have the new pairs, in different parts of the room, carry on ten-minute conversations, with freedom to turn to the observers for counsel.

6) Review in the whole group the conversations and compare them with the first. Which went more easily? Why? In which did participants learn more about each other? Why? Is there special value in coming to know a person rather different from oneself? What value?[2]

EXERCISE III. Your Name

Purpose: To explore the self-image and its relation to names as symbols.

Directions:

1) Begin with one member who will volunteer to be first. Have him do each of the following, observing and reporting feelings aroused.

    a) Go the board (or easel) and write your whole name. Tell a little of how you feel about each part of it as you write it.

    b) Let the whole group shout your name loudly in unison: first name, seven times; middle name, seven times; last name, seven times. How did this make you feel? (This step and the next one may be omitted if you feel they would be awkward for or not meaningful to your group.)

    c) Choose another member to stand near you and to whisper your preferred name gently, seven times.

    d) Tell the group any memories you have about reaction to your name. Does it seem to you to fit the real person you are? Why or why not?

    e) What first name (or nickname) would you choose if you were completely free to choose any name which best fits the kind of person you are? Would you like to experiment with having everyone call you by that new name for one day, or for several days?

2) Repeat with other group members until all have had their turn.

3) Save about ten minutes, more or less, for a group review of the exercise. Do names have anything to do with our self-image? What did you learn about the others as they talked about their names? [3]

EXERCISE IV. Sharing Past Histories

Purpose: To enable persons to share with each other a personal level of their lives.

Directions:

1) Ask each person to introduce himself by relating a significant personal experience which helped shape him into the person he is today. The experience could be from childhood, adolescence, or adult life. It could be religious or secular, joyful or painful. Especially in new groups it would be helpful for one of the leaders to begin this process. Ask participants to listen well, since they will need to remember what they hear.

2) Ask persons to break into pairs. If you are working with an "old" group, they should try to team up with persons they know the least. If it is a newly formed group, each person might like to select another who seems most different from himself.

3) In pairs, each person should repeat to the other's satisfaction what he heard the other say, including not only content but observations about feelings behind the actual words (what he thought the person felt about what he said). Allow about ten to fifteen minutes for this process.

4) In the large group, reflect upon what has happened in the process. How did participants feel about sharing themselves in

this manner? How did they feel as another person reflected on their experiences? What did they learn through the process?

NOTE: This exercise could be used fruitfully as you move through the entire study. Simply adapt it by changing the content to be shared. Ideas given in "Awareness Triggers" sections of the student's book would be appropriate sharing data.

EXERCISE V. Boundary Breaking

Purpose: 1) To begin group interaction from which a sense of community can be developed.

2) To create an awareness of the other person through the use of questions designed to reveal more than superficial conversations do.

3) To listen, knowing that listening is basic to learning about the other person.

Directions:

1) Ask each question below to each person in turn. Questions are not to be explained. If a person does not understand a question, repeat it with the same wording. Tell each person just to respond to what he hears. He should answer as simply as possible, without explaining his answer. The mood is to be kept serious at all times. If someone gives a flip, humorous answer, you may need to remind the group of this fact. Indicate that we are here to listen. We are not here to debate (this is urgent). We are not here to disagree. As each person answers, collect the answers in your head—develop an idea of each person. After a number of questions from the first set have been answered by all and while interest is still strong, switch to the synthesis set below without telling participants about the set beforehand. These questions ask a good bit of participants. If you do not feel your group is ready to engage in this kind of honest interaction, you could follow the procedure suggested in No. 2 of this exercise.

Questions for structured conversation:

a) Who is the person most relevant to our time?

b) When you think of reality, what comes to your mind first?

c) What is the most beautiful thing about people?

d) What physical thing do you want to build more than anything else?

e) What is the most sacred thing you know?

f) What is the ugliest thing you know?

g) What event of the last three months stands out in your mind the most?

h) On what basis do you select your friends?

i) What is the greatest value that guides your life?

j) If you could be any animal other than a human being, what animal would you choose to be?

k) If you could smash one thing and only one thing, what would you smash?

l) What is the greatest crime one person can do toward another?

m) If the atomic bomb was going to fall in ten minutes, what would you do in that last ten minutes?

n) Select a word that best describes your total life at this moment of time.

o) What do you think people like in you the least?

p) What do you think people like in you the most?

q) What would you like to be talented at that you are not at the present time?

r) What person has most influenced your life?

s) When do you feel most lonely?

t) When do you sense being alive the most?

u) What is your greatest fear?

v) What do you cherish the most?

w) If you had to use another word for God, what word would you use?

x) What one day in your life would you like to live over?

y) What is the most powerful force loose in the world today?

Synthesis set. (Answer these questions in light of the answers given by the group members.)

a) Which person did you learn the most about?

b) Which person did you think was most honest?

c) Which person did you think hid himself from you the most?

d) Which person do you think you could get along with best over a long period of time?

e) Which answer surprised you the most?

f) Which person seemed most sensitive to life?

g) Which person seems to enjoy life the most?

h) Which person do you feel is most like you?

i) Which person do you feel is least like you?

j) Which person would you go to if you needed help?

You may create alternate questions for your group, questions more in harmony with your group.[4]

2) Was this question-answer procedure a helpful means for gaining knowledge of others? Why, or why not? What would have helped us know more of each other in this brief period of time? Why? As participants interact, you will need to ask other questions related to their comments.

EXERCISE VI. SELF-PORTRAIT

There is the possibility of assigning this exercise as a home-work project if time is limited. Then step 3 could be done in your next session.

Purpose: 1) To enable persons to present themselves to others.

2) To enable persons to hear others say something significant about themselves.

Directions:

1) Have materials (a large number of old magazines, scissors, glue, posterboard or large newsprint) available for use in class.

2) If participants have read the first section of the student's book, ask them to reflect on thoughts they had about themselves as they did so. Then ask them to create two collages with clippings they find in the magazines. The first one should indicate the many selves they see operating in their person, the desires they have, the pressures they feel (conflicting selves). The second should communicate something they feel about their innermost self, how they see what they most truly *are*.

If members have had no opportunity for reading the book, ask them to in some way depict their own life as they now feel it to be. Let the collage communicate an answer to the question, Who am I?

Although you should indicate to the group that there is no right way to create a collage, it may be helpful to say, "Just start thumbing through a magazine, clipping or tearing out any picture, object, color, or words that seem to say something to you or about you. Then combine them in any way you please on the paper to make a statement about yourself."

You could have felt pens or crayons available in case someone prefers to do a drawing.

3) If time is limited, let the group divide into trios to present their portraits for discussion and explanation. It would, however, be of benefit to the entire group if each person who desires to would show his creation to the total group and make any explanation or comment he desires. The group should also be free to ask questions for clarification.

The following exercise could be used with *groups that have had some past experiences together*. This exercise could also be used in a retreat setting for newly formed groups toward the end of the retreat.

EXERCISE VII. Perceptions of Each Other

Purpose: 1) To share with others through images and analogies our view of ourselves and others.

2) To listen to others' views through images and analogies.

3) To understand that individuals perceive differently.

4) To see how different perceptions bring different responses.

Directions:

1) Take a few minutes for each individual to think of himself and of each member of the group in a metaphor or image—as a color, an animal, a car, a song, a picture, etc.

2) Then allow members of the group to share their perception of each member of the group in turn. Before moving to the next person, allow the person to give his own perception of himself. As persons describe their images of themselves or others, they should include in the description what meaning it has for them, how they feel about it, etc. As you can see, this will be a lengthy process, and it should be loosely organized. Each person should feel free to withhold his perception if it is repetitious of another's or if he does not want to share this information. You may not have time for sharing all perceptions, but be sure that each participant receives a few perceptions of himself from others.

3) When the sharing is completed, allow members to express their thoughts and feelings about what has happened.

Closing the First Session

After the group experience, if it seems appropriate, close the session with a prayer of thanksgiving for the uniqueness of individuals and for the gifts from each person which have been shared within the group during the session.

If your group is an "old" group, you may want to consider distributing handout sheets of "Patterns of Interpersonal Relationship," page 125. Both newly formed and old groups might benefit from the study of "Awareness and Sensitivity in Interpersonal Relations," page 135.

Assignment

If participants have not done so, ask them to study the student's book through chapter 2.

Session

2

Purpose: To provide one or more class experiences through which participants may
1) grow in awareness and knowledge of each other;
2) express care, respect, and concern for one another;
3) explore some truths related to the meaning of the activity called love.

Directions

You will want to continue with a room arrangement conducive to a free, open, warm interchange between persons. As you select an exercise or exercises for this session keep the following considerations in mind: (1) What kind of group life has been established up to this point? Do group members seem to have some feeling of community? Was there freedom for self-giving and receiving in the past session? Are more introductory types of activities needed? If so, you may want to select an exercise from the previous session. (2) Be particularly aware of individual needs, strengths, etc., observed in your last session which might enter into your selection of activities. Were there individuals who seemed uncomfortable or hesitant? What exercises might they enter into most easily? Were there persons who seemed particularly free and enthusiastic? Could they be called upon to start a particular exercise? How can their strengths be helpful to the group? Simply review in your mind what happened in the last session and see what it suggests as you read and think through possible exercises, discussion, Bible study, or theory sessions. (3) According to what actually happened in your last meeting, select an activity which seems to be a follow-up and will be a step further toward establishing deeper group life.

Be aware of the fact that the purpose of these sessions is not to cover in a comprehensive manner any particular subject (in this session, love). Rather, it is to provide an experience which speaks to some aspect of the loving relationship. This experience is seen only as a spark to ignite deeper self-awareness, awareness of others, and some aspects of what happens as human beings relate to one another. Trust the individual to go on from there. If he becomes really involved, he will discover truths which can have life-changing value for him. All the beautiful, true words in the world might not have this effect. As a teacher, I find this the hardest lesson of all to learn. I find myself wanting to say everything I know or have discovered. I want to explore with students every possible aspect of truth. Then I feel that I have accomplished my task. But I am learning that the person discovers, explores, and applies truth *as he experiences it* rather than as he hears "all my wonderful words." I am also learning that any area of truth dealt with in class is only the beginning of a lifelong process in which the individual person continues to learn and discover. I no longer have to "say it all," or even to see that "all of it" is explored. A spark of experienced learning can start a fire. A rock thrown in the water sends ever expanding rings further and further from the point of impact.

EXERCISES

EXERCISE I. The Johari Window (high risk)

This exercise is related to the Johari Window described in the resource section, page 135, "Awareness and Sensitivity in Interpersonal Relations."

Purpose: 1) To enable individuals to share something of themselves so that others may grow in understanding of that individual.

2) To enable individuals to receive knowledge of themselves through feedback.

Directions:

1) If participants have not been previously introduced to the Johari Window, prepare a brief lecture presenting the central factors needed to understand the concept. The exercise is designed to show how a group can enlarge the area of free communication for all its members.

2) Ask for a volunteer to exchange an item of his "hidden" area for an item from his "blind" area. According to where your group is and which in your judgment seems best, ask the volunteer to present one of the following:

a) something about himself which he feels is important—it may even be something he has never told anyone before;

b) some life experience, not previously shared with the group, which had a profound and life-changing effect upon his life; or

c) some life experience which taught him something about the meaning of love (a relationship which caused him to be more loving, a relationship which taught him what love is not).

3) After the volunteer has shared something of himself, he is "rewarded" by hearing something that other group members have observed or felt about him of which he is probably unaware. It is most likely to be helpful if it is an observation that one does not ordinarily tell another. This does not imply that it must be unpleasant, or critical in a negative sense, for we often withhold our very positive feelings from one another. You may want to remind the group that as the volunteer shares something of himself, the group should be receptive listeners, not judging but simply trying to put themselves in the volunteer's shoes, *feeling* what he is saying from his world of experience. You might suggest that, if possible, the information given from the "blind" area should be related to the information shared by the volunteer. For example, if the volunteer shared an experience that taught him something about love, the shared information might be some observation about the volunteer that indicates a strength he has to share in a love relationship, or some quality of life he communicates that draws others to him, or some characteristic that may cause others to be fearful of him, etc.

4) After the first exchange, ask for another volunteer to offer something from his hidden area in exchange for an item from his blind area. No participants should be compelled to participate, but no one should be allowed a second exchange until every member who wants to has shared something about himself. After all who desire to have shared one experience, the exercise could continue for two or three rounds.

5) Close the exercise by taking ten to fifteen minutes for the group to discuss what has happened during this time of shared life. Do any members have different *feelings* toward others? What are they? What is the atmosphere within the group as a result of the giving and receiving? What created this atmosphere? If participants answer in generalities, ask them to be more specific. For example, if someone says, "I feel closer to everyone in the group,"

you might ask, "In what ways do you feel closer? What exactly caused you to feel this way?" [1]

NOTE: Remember that this exercise cannot fail! If there should be no volunteers, explore with the group the reality of the situation. No one feels free to give of his hidden area within this particular group. Why do we feel that way? Do we fear each other? Do we fear the reactions of others? What is needed in our group so that we can be more truly ourselves with each other? Or do we feel that we should not reveal areas of ourselves which we have previously withheld from others? What is behind this feeling?

Of if the activity moves for a while but seems to have little meaning for the group, stop and explore with the group what is happening, why it is happening, and the meaning of this for group life.

A variation of this exercise would be to break into pairs or trios for the sharing of hidden and blind areas, then bring the smaller groupings back together for step 5. This variation might be more easily entered into by groups who do not yet feel at home with each other.

EXERCISE II. People Need People

This exercise should be used only with a group whose members have a fair knowledge of one another. If your group is a newly formed one, consider using it later in the life of your group.

Purpose: To enable participants to explore and acknowledge
1) their need for other people;
2) the gifts they have to share with others.

Directions:

1) Have the quotations below printed on posterboard and displayed so they can be seen by all participants. Ask members simply to reflect on their meaning for a few minutes. *Do not* get into a discussion of the quotations. Distribute pencil and paper.

Then the LORD God said,
"It is not good for the man to be alone."
[Gen. 2:18, N.E.B.]

No person is self-reliant,
And when a person allows another
to supplement his lack,
he makes friendship and love possible.[2]

Always there remains this need
to explain to each other
that we are good. We all have a
constant need to be reaffirmed.
The single man needs this.
The whole human race needs a yea,
needs the large ceremonial
pat on the back that says
Come on, come on! We can make it.[3]

We need
to have people
who mean something
to us.
People
to whom
we can turn
knowing
that being with them
is coming Home.[4]

2) Ask each person to make a list of needs he has which can be filled by other persons, needs which may prevent him from living as fully as he might. Indicate that this list will not be made public unless he chooses to make it so. (Allow about five minutes.)

3) Ask each to look at his list of people-needs, and then to look around the room from person to person and jot down one

need on his list which he feels each particular person could help meet. This list should be as specific as possible. The person should ask himself, "Knowing what I do about that person, or perceiving this or that potentiality in that person, what could he do for me?" Indicate that statements similar to the following are too general: "John could meet a need for friendship." What in John makes friendship seem possible or appealing? Is it his quick wit, his ability to listen, his warmth, his intellectual understanding, his trustworthiness, or what?

4) Allow those who are willing to share with the group their second listing to do so. The volunteers should be asked to look at the person as he tells him what personal need he feels the person could meet.

5) Now ask each person to imagine that he is a Santa Claus who has just descended the chimney but has lost his bag of gifts in the process. What can you now give to each person in this group? What do you have to share? How would you give it? Allow a few minutes for each person to think about gifts he has to give to meet various individual's needs as he perceives them.

6) Ask those who are willing to do so to move from person to person in the group, telling each whatever comes spontaneously to mind as a gift they can give to that person.

7) Spend ten to fifteen minutes reflecting upon what happened as you thought about the human need for giving to and receiving from others. How do people feel about what happened? Did anyone become more aware of a strength he has as a result of another's perception of him? As people talked about their needs, did anyone grow in awareness of human gifts he has to give? Did anyone become more aware of his own needs for people and of ways in which others could help him have a fuller life? Questions will need to be geared to the particular experience your group had, of course.

EXERCISE III. Role Play

Purpose: 1) To gain a fresh awareness of the fact that love is a difficult art.

2) To enable participants to wrestle with ways of expressing respect, care, and responsibility in strained relationships.

Directions:

The central thrust of this role play will be to get inside of and "feel" a relationship in which it is difficult to express love. Each person in the role play should be asked to put himself "inside the skin" of the person whose role he is assuming, to walk around in it, and to act spontaneously *as* that person. Below you will find a possible role-play situation, but you or your group may want to select another that will have more meaning for your group. If so, (1) choose a typical personal problem in which love relationships are strained. In this particular exercise, since you are using it to help people become aware of the difficulties in loving, rather than just learning how it feels to be another person, be sure that the problem is one with which participants can identify. Observers should be asked to select one role portrayed and to try to feel with that role. (2) Select a setting or situation for the problem, deciding who, where, when, how to begin.

Possible Problem. A mother has found the following rough draft of a letter from her son to a friend he met during summer camp. She shares its content with her husband and they decide to try to talk things out with their son after supper. They want a deeper, more honest relationship with their son.

> *Letter:* "Well, I'm alive, and things are looking good. I never knew I could be so happy about just being alive, but I am. I miss all of you, but I can't depend on you. *I have to look to myself.* I'm determined not to waste this year; I

mean I don't know how many there are left, but I want to live, I mean really live, meeting people, having fun, giving.

"I've finally hit on the right relationship with my parents. A lonely one, but I know it's right. It's one that entails nothing deep, not kidding around, not being close, but just being polite and giving them no reason to complain, and living my life to the fullest in all ways. It's working, but I miss them." [5]

Setting. After finishing supper the son, Rob, asks for the family car to go see some friends and the father refuses, saying he feels it is the time to get some things straightened out.

1) After you decide on the situation, ask for or select persons to act out necessary roles. Before action begins, ask persons who will take the roles to silently consider questions such as: If you are the father, what is your job? What are some of your interests? How do you feel about your son? Were you close to him when he was younger? How did you feel when he started growing up? What are your hopes for his future? Do you really like him now? The mother should consider similar questions. The person taking the role of the son should identify how the person writing the letter felt. What led him to the relationship he now considers as a right one with his parents? What made him feel so good at camp? Why does he feel there may not be many years left?

These questions are seen as mood-setting ones to help persons get inside the roles. They should not be answered orally, but simply pondered. If you select another situation, ask participants to think through similar questions related to the roles in the situation.

2) Arrange as simple a setting as possible: tables, chairs, telephone—any prop essential to the action.

3) Start the action. Participants talk and act spontaneously, responding to each other as dialogue develops. Cut after four

to ten minutes when respective attitudes and behaviors have been clearly seen.

4) Discuss and evaluate what went on. How did the participants feel? What made showing love and concern difficult in the situation? What changes within a person or within a relationship are necessary for a deeper understanding to come about? How did observers feel about what happened? What changes would they make if they were the persons in the situation?

5) Change characters and replay the situation to see how new participants will cope with the difficulties. This might be done several times if it seems profitable.

6) Discuss what has been observed as persons have acted and reacted to each other in the situation. What barriers to love have been seen? What helpful, uniting actions and reactions were seen? What made these possible? What feeling brought about acts which hindered loving relationships? Be sure to relate all answers to what actually happened in the role play.

A Variation. At some point in the role play, you might include six people in the situation: one to act out what the son says and does and a second son, an alter ego, to say what the son is thinking as he talks and reacts to his parents. Provide egos and alter egos for the mother and father also. If you use this variation, at the end raise questions such as: Would it be good if these two aspects of the person were one? What would happen? How can they become one?

EXERCISE IV. Caring Respect

Purpose: 1) To create a situation in which the nature and importance of respect and concern for others can be explored.

2) To enable persons to feel what it is like not to be respected.

3) To enable persons to become aware of what kinds of feelings and reactions lack of respect brings forth in them.

Directions:

1) Select a person who has the understanding, knowledge, and ability to present a meaningful lecture on the subject of love, and ask him if he will help you with an experiment in your class. Announce to the class that the person (ideally someone class members do not know) will speak on "Love and How We Can Become More Loving."

2) Instruct the speaker to plan the beginning of a lecture on the topic and to present that beginning to the class in as unloving, insulting, and disrespectful a manner as possible. For example, he might begin by saying, "I'm sure that what I have to say about love really won't make much difference in your lives since no one today really cares about anyone except themselves. But I'll try anyway." He might continue with the lecture, interspersing comments such as: "I know you businessmen don't think you have time to worry or care about others. All you are concerned with is profit for yourselves and getting ahead." Or, "Most of you ladies can't take time out from your social life to really risk showing deep love to your family." Or, "I'll bet your major concern with your children is what kinds of grades they are making, or whether they seem to be credits to their family. You don't really care about their personal growth." Or, "I know you church people talk a lot about love, but you do very little of it." And so forth, according to what would be appropriate to your group. However, when the speaker interjects comments similar to those above, he should not be too obvious about what he is doing.

3) After the speaker has aroused sufficient feelings in the class members (and before active hostility breaks out), interrupt

the lecture and explain that the whole speech was a staged event to give the class an immediate experience of how it feels to be treated in a disrespectful, uncaring, distrustful manner. Give participants five minutes to jot down what they were feeling during the lecture.

4) Begin discussion by asking class members to share their feelings. It would be helpful if the guest speaker could stay and join in the discussion. As discussion proceeds, interject questions to keep it focused upon what lack of loving, understanding concern and respect do to people. What feelings and reactions are aroused in people? What kind of atmosphere is created? How does it make people feel about themselves and others? How does it affect their perception of what they hear and see? How does it affect what they do?

You might then move to general consideration of the positive aspects of respect and understanding concern for others by questions such as: What happens in you when you are in a situation where you know someone respects you as a unique individual who is of great value? How do you respond to such a person? What feelings does such a person call forth in you? [6]

Assignment

Ask participants to study chapter 3 in the student's book. If you did not distribute the suggested handout sheets in your last session, you might consider doing so.

Session
3

Purpose: To provide opportunity for persons to become more aware of and/or learn and practice
  1) skills which will help them become more sensitive to life in and around them; and
  2) skills of verbal and nonverbal communication.

EXERCISE I. Eye Contact—Strength Bombardment

Purpose: 1) To become more aware of eye communication.
  2) To affirm and strengthen individuals.

Directions:

1) Divide the participants into groups of four to eight persons each. Place a volunteer from each group in the center of his group. In turn, each member of the group is to place his hands on the shoulders of the volunteer and for twenty or thirty seconds to look directly into the eyes of the volunteer to find something good there, something he likes and can affirm. After each person has had his turn, the volunteer is asked to turn his back to the group, and the group members tell the good and positive feelings they had, the qualities they saw which they can affirm in that person.

2) Call the group back together and discuss questions similar to the following. To the volunteer: What were your feelings as you looked into the eyes of others? What were your feelings as others discussed your qualities? To group members: What did you feel as you experienced eye-to-eye contact with the volunteer?

What were your feelings as you discussed a person who was present but not a part of the conversation? What have we learned about communication?

3) According to what was actually experienced, you might want to move to this third step. You will need to decide on the basis of where your group is at this time. Have the quotation below read and then discussed.

> The lover perceives in the beloved what no one else can, and again, there is no question about the intrinsic value of his inner experience and of the many good consequences for him, for his beloved, and for the world. If we take as an example the mother loving her baby, the case is even more obvious. Not only does love perceive potentialities but it also actualizes them. The absence of love certainly stifles potentialities and even kills them. Personal growth demands courage, self-confidence, even daring; and non-love from the parent or the mate produces the opposite, self-doubt, anxiety, feelings of worthlessness and expectation of ridicule, all inhibitors of growth and of self-actualization.
> All personological and psychotherapeutic experience is testimonial to this fact that love actualizes and non-love stultifies, whether deserved or not.[1]

Discuss questions such as: Did we experience any part of the truth Maslow is referring to? Did individuals being affirmed experience a surge of self-confidence and/or courage? Do you feel strengthened for growth?

4) You could then ask if individuals would share personal experiences in which they have felt love or the absence of love calling forth or stifling potentialities within them. Allow as many to share experiences as seems helpful.

EXERCISE II. Hearing Through Nonverbal Communication

Purpose: 1) To help persons become more aware of and sensitive to nonverbal communication.

2) To allow persons to share themselves with others.

Directions:

1) Place chairs for half the group in a circle. Half of the group should be seated and half should stand, each behind a chair in the circle. Each standing person becomes the partner of the seated person facing him (directly across the circle from him).

2) Each seated person is asked to share briefly with the group a childhood relationship which he views as one that strengthened him and helped him develop some potentiality within him.

3) As each person shares his chosen experience, the partner outside the circle is asked to cover his ears as his partner speaks. The partner outside should be as observant as possible of non-verbal communication—position of head and body, movements of hands and head, facial expressions, eyes, breathing.

4) After every seated person has shared an experience, positions should be reversed. The persons now seated should with closed eyes share a childhood relationship which they feel was a strengthening one. The partner outside *listens* and *observes.*

5) After all seated persons have spoken, have partners get together and share what has just happened. What did each see and/or hear as the other spoke through verbal and nonverbal means? What feelings seemed to come through beneath the spoken and unspoken communication? How did the observer feel when he could see and not hear what was being communicated? Was he able to understand the content of what was said? What did we learn about communication?

6) Bring the pairs back together in a large group to see if there are learnings individuals would like to share with the total group.

EXERCISE III. Empathy

Purpose: 1) To identify how we can feel *with* others.

   2) To try and understand what it must be like to be another person.

3) To see the world through the eyes of another person.

4) To realize and celebrate the fact that each person is unique, a person who is a particular child of God.

Directions:

1) Each member of the group is given a lemon (oranges or something else similar may be used). Lemons can be in a bag and each person selects his own.

2) Tell each person to look at his lemon very carefully. Get acquainted with it. Feel what it would be like to be inside. Smell it, touch it, heft it. Get to know it as best you can. Talk about your lemon one at a time out loud. Give it a name; tell something about your lemon—its position, likes, dislikes, etc.

3) Put all the lemons in a pile or in a box. Mix them up.

4) Have each person, one at a time, go to the pile and pick out his own lemon.

5) Have each person share his feelings about what just happened. Ask, "How were you able to pick out your lemon?" What does the exercise say about our ability to "be in the shoes" of another person? Are we all alike? What are some of the implications of this exercise for such statements as: All whites (or blacks) look alike. All youth (or parents) are alike. How can we use this experience to know each other better as individuals rather than by labels?[2]

EXERCISE IV. Awareness

Purpose: 1) To illustrate in an experimental manner the fact that most of us are not nearly as aware of our surroundings as we think.

2) To become aware of the value of fuller use of our senses.

3) To find ways of cultivating sensory awareness.

Directions:

1) Bring to class a small container of mustard or other objects which can be smelled, a piece of paper cut from an ordinary paper bag, and a piece of any available common kind of cloth.

2) Have the group divide into pairs, seated next to each other. One member of the pair should take part in the exercise; the other should be instructed to record the participant's answers on a sheet of paper.

3) Tell participants to close their eyes and then answer a series of questions. If their answer is a guess, they should indicate this to their partner, who is keeping "score."

   a) What is the color of the walls of the room? (Or pick out some other dominant item like draperies, bulletin board, chairs.)

   b) What color are my eyes?

   c) Is _____ (some group member) wearing a (coat, hat, or whatever seems appropriate to ask)?

   d) Ask them to feel the piece of paper you prepared and tell them they have probably felt this kind of paper within the last few days. Can they identify what kind of paper it is or where they felt it?

   e) Ask them to identify the piece of cloth, indicating that it is a common kind.

   f) Ask them to stop and listen for two full minutes to see how many sounds they can identify. Ask the partner to record the number. Compare kinds and numbers of sounds recognized at this time.

   g) Ask them to identify the odor you present to them. (Circulate mustard or other objects you brought.)

4) Now ask partners to reverse roles. Explain that everyone should try to observe as many things as they can in the room— colors, objects, persons—within a set time (about two minutes).

5) Now ask new participants to close their eyes as their partner records their answers. Ask specific questions about the room and individual persons. Continue this for a few minutes or until the participants get some feel of how observant or unobservant they are. Sample questions are:

      a) What kind of shoes is _____ wearing?
      b) How many pictures are on the walls?
      c) What color is _____'s shirt?
      d) Where are the electrical outlets located? the heating outlets?
      e) What color is the floor? the ceiling?

6) Allow a few minutes for partners to exchange results of this experience. Then enter into a general discussion of what has happened by questions similar to the following: How did you feel when you realized you couldn't answer some of the questions? Were you surprised at the number of sounds you heard when you really stopped to listen? Why don't we tend to notice things like sounds, color of a person's eyes, articles of clothing, how things feel? Are you aware of what's in your home—the colors, the odors, the sounds, the feel of things, unique things about the people? Do you know the color of each person's eyes? Are these things really important? Do you feel more, or less, "alive" when you are very much aware of things and people around you? Why? How do you feel when someone takes notice of a physical characteristic, what you are wearing, how you are feeling, or the things you say? Why? Why do artists (visual, literary, musical) tend to notice all kinds of little things that others overlook? What effect does it have on them? What effect does this kind of noticing have on human relationships (how we treat one another)? How important is it in the communication process? If you want to develop an ability to be more aware of all that is going on around you, what are some ways you might do it? If you have time, experiment with some of the things suggested.[3]

During this discussion you might want to have some of the statements about sensitivity from the participant's text, pages 66–67, 74–76, available for discussion at particular points.

EXERCISE V. Expressive Behavior

Use one or more of the suggestions for expressive behavior on page 140. Although this kind of expression is difficult for some persons, if your group is willing to experiment, expressive behavior can be freeing and helpful in making us more aware of nonverbal means of communication. If you use these suggestions, follow them with questions which allow participants to say how they felt, what they experienced, and what they learned about themselves, about others, and about the use of the body as a means of communication.

EXERCISE VI. Body Talk

The simulation game *Body Talk,* published by *Psychology Today,* was created to help persons learn to use their bodies as effective, conscious communicators. It would be an excellent tool for use in this session.

Assignment

Ask students to study chapter 4. You might also consider duplicating for distribution to class members "The Helping Relationship and Feedback," page 120.

Session

4

Purpose: To provide opportunity for persons to
1) identify various levels of communication;
2) evaluate the level or levels at which they generally communicate; and
3) experiment with "intimate" communication.

You may not be able to accomplish every aspect of this purpose in one session. If you have only one, identify the needs of your group and choose an exercise accordingly. Of course, you will need to practice this sort of judgment in all sessions which follow.

EXERCISE I. Love and Communication

Purpose: To provide an opportunity for participants to
1) discuss a statement about love;
2) observe and identify various levels of communication.

Directions:

1) Divide the participants into two groups. One group should take part in a discussion, while the others observe group interaction. Ask each observer to select one person, perhaps the one across from and facing him, to be especially aware of.

2) Ask discussants to explore the meaning of this statement: "Our lives are shaped by those who love us—by those who refuse to love us." Have the statement on posterboard or on the chalkboard for all to see. Allow the discussion to extend ten to fifteen minutes, according to how it is going.

3) Now ask everyone to look at the five levels of communication—trivial prattle, monologues, everyday conversation, creative dialogue, and intimacy (student's book, pp. 58–60)—and list them for all to see. Then ask observers to identify the kinds of communication they saw occurring. You may need to remind the group that in making observations no judgments are to be made. Members are simply to identify what actually occurred. As observations are made, persons commented about may want to say how they saw their level of communication. Encourage discussion about any nonverbal communication which occurred during the exchange. If there were no exchanges at the level of intimacy, the group may try to see why. If there was sharing at this level, try to understand what elements in the situation freed persons for this kind of dialogue. All discussion should be about specifics observed.

4) If there is time, the groups could exchange places. The new group could discuss the following: "The day I found self-respect was the day I discovered I *am* something to give to others."

5) After the second round of discussion and observations, compare the two rounds. If there were differences in levels of communication, how do you account for them?

EXERCISE II. Significant Sharing

Purpose: 1) To offer opportunity for sharing significant experiences at whatever level of communication persons choose.

2) To gain insight into one's present feelings and behavior.

3) To offer opportunity for revising one's self-image.

Directions:

1) In a three-round session, participants are given the opportunity to share an earlier experience which they see to be signifi-

cant *and related to* the following statement: "Our lives are shaped by those who love us—by those who refuse to love us."

Each participant should be prepared to explain how he thinks the experience he describes actually affected him. Ask participants to limit accounts to one to three minutes.

Round 1—Sharing a significant experience from the first ten years of life.

Round 2—An important event during teen-age years.

Round 3—A life-changing event from adult life.

2) Divide the participants into groups of three or four persons, assigning them the task of exploring what has been shared. Which members of the smaller groups seem to have been most affected by an experience from childhood? adolescence? adulthood? What feelings were conveyed during the sharing of experiences? What content was expressed through nonverbal means? Members of the small groups should also help each other look at possible present effects (attitudes, feelings, and actions) caused by these significant events. Can individuals see any of their present feelings and reactions being repeats of earlier responses described? Do these findings say anything about the person's present self-image or feelings?

EXERCISE III. Creative Listening

Purpose: 1) To allow participants to share something they would like to with another.

2) To allow participants to engage in a listening activity so that they can see how well they listen.

3) To discover the importance of creative listening.

Directions:

1) Divide the participants into pairs and explain that each person is to take turns listening while the other person tells some-

thing he has discovered about himself during this study. He could describe his present self-image, some mask he wears he would like to rid himself of, some area in which he would like to bring about change—anything he would like to communicate at any level of communication.

2) Announce that each person will be given three minutes to share whatever he would like. During this time the listener should not ask questions or interrupt in any manner. He should strive to be aware of nonverbal as well as verbal communication. It would be helpful for you to watch the time and after three minutes to tell pairs to change roles for another three minutes.

3) At the end of the second three minutes, tell the teams to test how well they listened. Based on what they heard, one person is to tell his partner how he thinks that person *feels* about what he said. (What seemed to be the most important aspect of what he said? the most difficult to tell about? What emotions did he seem to experience as he talked? Why did the listener think he was feeling these emotions? When this is finished, the partner should judge how accurate the listener was. He might also see whether the listener picked up some aspect of the situation or problem which had not been in the full awareness of the speaker. Then roles are reversed for the second period.

4) If there is time, repeat the whole process.

5) Ask the entire group to come together to share their experiences. Questions such as the following might be helpful: What did you learn through this exercise? What did you discover about communication—talking, listening, dialoguing? How does careful listening affect your willingness or ability to communicate? Did you find out anything about how difficult it is to convey exact meanings, as you heard your partner report what he thought you felt? It has been said that better listening, not talking, is the first

step in good communication. Does your experience validate or negate this statement? Explain. Gear your questions to the kind of experiences described.[1]

NOTE: The procedure used in this exercise could be easily adapted for use in other sessions. The "Awareness Triggers" sections may provide ideas for a variety of data that might be shared.

EXERCISE IV. Loneliness and the Capacity to Love

Purpose: To provide a stimulus situation which may allow persons to
1) identify experiences of anxiety created by loneliness;
2) explore ways of creatively confronting loneliness or "abandonment anxiety";
3) examine the level of communication taking place in class experience.

Directions:

1) Divide your class into groups of four to six. Ask someone to read aloud "Loneliness and the Capacity to Love," page 154.

2) Ask groups to spend five to ten minutes thinking about the questions following the statement (you might want to duplicate them).

3) Instruct group members to share with one another any experience of loneliness or of dealing with loneliness which comes to mind. Allow about fifteen minutes.

5) Now ask group members to examine what level of communication occurred during this exercise. If it was a rather surface level, revealing few feelings—why? If persons seemed free to share their whole selves, what made such communication possible?

6) Call groups together to share any findings about loneliness, the ability to deal with loneliness, the capacity for love, or communication.

Alternate Exercises

If you did not use the suggestions from Exercises V or VI from session 3, you could consider them for this session.

Assignment

Remind participants to follow through on "Suggestions for Thought and Action" in chapters 3 and 4 of the student's book.

Session

5

Purpose: To enable persons
  1) to identify causes of normal anxiety;
  2) to identify their reactions to normal anxiety; and
  3) to help them accept more fully the fact that anxiety is a part of human existence.

EXERCISE I. Anxiety, a Factor in Human Growth

Purpose: 1) To identify various life crises in an individual's development that caused anxiety.
  2) To explore the individual's way of dealing with anxiety.

Directions:

1) In three rounds individuals will be asked to recall and share past experiences of anxiety. In each round, each participant is asked to tell about some experience of normal anxiety from the suggested stage in his development. You might suggest the following "for instances" to start the recall process: your first day at school, your first night away from home, your first date, a big misunderstanding with a trusted friend or your family, going away to college, your marriage, a vocational decision, or some work responsibility.

Then ask each how he thinks this experience affected him. Did it free him and give him courage for the next time he met a new or threatening situation, or did it cause him to be more fearful of life? Each person should take no more than three minutes for his recall. At the end of each round, allow time for the group to share and explore any general understandings about anxiety common to a particular stage of development.

Round 1—A childhood experience.
Round 2—An experience from adolescence.
Round 3—An experience from adult life.

2) Ask participants to share feelings they had as they told and listened to anxiety-producing situations. Did anyone notice in themselves or others any physical reactions to the subject matter? What nonverbal means of communication were observed? How do participants feel now?

3) What experiences related revealed constructive means of meeting anxiety-producing situations? That is, what experiences seemed to free the individual to move on to greater freedom and fuller development of his capacities? What experiences had negative effects on the person—that is, caused him to pull back from life or to see various aspects of life as threatening?

4) If there is time, participants might share any thoughts they have in answer to the question, To what extent do your present feelings, attitudes, and acts repeat these earlier reactions? If time has run out, simply ask class members to think about the question.

EXERCISE II. Anxiety as a Threat to a Common Value
(high risk)

Purpose: To enable participants to
1) observe an anxiety-producing situation;
2) experience anxiety rising in themselves;
3) identify and explore various reactions to anxiety.

If you have courage to risk whatever happens, and if you know a person or persons who would be willing to take a risk with you, try this.

Directions:

1) Identify some value generally accepted and cherished by class members—for example, patriotism, family love, the validity of the Christian faith, the work of your particular congregation, respect for you as a person. You know your group. Ask yourself, "What value if attacked would create anxiety within my class?" The answer may suggest a situation for your class. Then decide how you could create within the class session a genuine conflict situation centered on that value. Who would be good to help you? According to the value area selected, decide whether an outsider (someone you work with, from your family, the minister) or someone from the class could best help you in the experiment.

2) With the help of the person or persons you selected, plan details about how to proceed. The following account of an actual classroom situation will suggest possibilities to you. In planning a learning situation for a group involved in a study of the prophets, my brother and I decided upon the following procedure. I began the class session by giving the historical background for the time of Isaiah. At the appointed time, my brother burst into the room and in true prophetic fashion started verbally attacking me as a representative of the institutional church. In the exchange which followed, he pointed to such things as the hypocrisy of church members, who talk and learn a great deal about love but only enter into superficial expressions of living that love. His attack was made very specific by pointing to such things as the once-a-week recreational program the group provided in an underprivileged area, the fact that the group did nothing to change the basic living conditions of the children in the recreational program, and the fact that the group returned after the recreational program to plush living conditions, feeling warmed and comforted by their own "good deeds" and forgetting about the hard realities of the lives of the children. As the session proceeded, my brother and I

simply responded to each other within the assumed roles. His role was that of the prophet pointing to the hypocrisy apparent in the life of the church. My role was simply my own. The role play was cut after about fifteen minutes. Then the class looked at what had happened.

Although this session was planned for an experience of some aspects of the prophetic function, the experience produced varying degrees of anxiety within the role-play participants and the class members. You will want to plan a situation which will allow you to explore anxiety experienced during the role play when a way of life or a value with which class participants identify is threatened. The antagonist in your situation will need to think through valid attacks on the value area chosen. Unless he is really able to "endanger" the validity of the value at stake, participants will have no deep reaction to the situation.

A possible way for starting your session would be to ask members how they are getting along with the work-study sections in their study book. Are they finding time to do any of the work? Are they finding it helpful? Have they altered the suggestions to fit their own lives? Are they able to carry over learnings into into their own lives? Such sharing could be beneficial. Individuals who have entered into constructive work on their own lives may offer encouragement to those who have had difficulty with the work-study sections or have seen no need for such work. (It would be good to explore the effectiveness of the work-study section at some point during the study, if you do not do so through this exercise.)

Plan when the person (persons) who is working with you will interrupt the session. You could set a specific time or you could give a signal. Then simply allow the situation to evolve. It is helpful to think through the general movement of the planned experience, the general way the persons in the roles feel and think, and the opening lines of each role. Then let the experience take its own shape as the "I" of the role interacts with the other "I." Too much detailed planning produces a staged, static, sterile effect, and prevents spontaneous, real-life action and interaction. Unless the situation is a realistic one in which a value is really threatened, no deep feelings will arise in the group. You could consider having the antagonist engage in interaction not only with you but also with the entire group for fuller group participation.

3) Cut the staged situation after five to fifteen minutes, depending upon what happens and the level of group involvement. If possible the role play should be stopped at the peak of involvement. Explain as briefly as possible the experiment and the reason for it. Then ask participants to quickly jot down what they were feeling just before you explained the situation. Ask them to record (1) how they were feeling in the situation, and (2) the causes of these feelings.

4) Allow class members to share what was going on inside them during the event. In the discussion which follows explore questions such as the following: What was threatening to you personally? Was this a realistic threat? That is, what would have happened to you if the antagonist was right? What was at stake? Was your perception always clear? Did you get personally involved at points where you were not personally being attacked? Did you feel hostile toward the antagonist? What caused this hostility? Do you feel strengthened or weakened by the experience? Why? What did it make you want to do? In thinking about the way you reacted, does this seem to be a typical reaction for you? To what extent do you think this reaction might reflect earlier responses in anxiety-producing situations?

These questions are only suggestive. Keeping in mind the purpose of the exercise, try to create your own questions in response to the information shared by members as they report what happened to them. The role players will also want to report their feelings. If they really get inside the roles, their reactions will tell them much about themselves.

EXERCISE III. Sharing Experiences of Anxiety

Adapt the exercise "Creative Listening" from session 4, page 64, for use in this session. Combine the method of sharing and listening used for that exercise with the purpose and questions used in Exercise I of this session. In the general discussion of the listening exercise, step 5, instead of exploring implications of the exercise for the process of communication, explore questions similar to those in steps 3–5 of Exercise I in this session.

EXERCISE IV. Anxiety Arising from a Threat to One's Life-Style

Purpose: To create a situation in which participants can
     1) experience anxious feelings arising in them;
     2) identify ways they respond to anxiety.

Directions:

1) Divide participants into two groups and have each group appoint a spokesman to represent it. Designate one group as representatives of the youth counter-culture and the other as representatives of the typical adult culture. Each group should make a conscious effort *really* to identify with the group they represent. (If this is not a live issue with your group, choose one that is—a stress which is present in society and which is keenly felt by members of your group.)

2) Explain that each group should take ten to fifteen minutes to list (a) three things they dislike most about the other group; (b) three things about the other group they simply cannot understand; (c) three reasons why they think the other group refuses to understand their viewpoint and/or refuses to change. If you do not think that adults in your group have an understanding of the youth culture, plan to be in that group yourself and do some prior study from *The Making of a Counter Culture* by Theodore

Roszak or a more current book or article. If you have young people in your group, let them assume their own role.

In this experiment, to really allow participants to get involved at a deep feeling level it might be helpful before class to ask one or two members of each group to work with you as antagonists. Their role will be (1) to express themselves as emotionally as possible; (2) to reflect a real lack of understanding of the other group (the kind of distorted perception of others which often occurs in real life); and (3) to show a real distrust of the other group. If they play their roles effectively, it will trigger a feeling-level involvement of other persons.

3) Bring groups back together, but still in separate "camps" (perhaps sitting across the room from each other). After the reports from each group, ask anyone who wants to from each group to respond to the charges of the other group. It is at this point that your planted people can be most effective. From there on, just see what happens in the next five to fifteen minutes.

4) Cut off the discussion, and tell the group to focus on what actually happened within and between persons during the experience. If the situation did evolve into one in which some participants actually experienced a threat to their way of life, ask them to report what they were feeling during the encounter. Then proceed to questions similar to those suggested in step 4 of Exercise II of this session. You will also want to identify the planted persons and to allow the group to explore what effect they had in the group experience.

If persons did not seem to get personally involved in the discussion, switch purposes and explore what did occur on an interpersonal level. Look at the level of communication. If it was a fairly superficial level, ask, "Why were we unwilling to enter into this exercise on a deeper level? What would have allowed for more personal involvement?" Or if there was a good bit of "gut-level" communication, explore what freed people for such exchanges. Did persons really listen to each other? Did they try to understand the other's viewpoint? Was there any evidence of distorted perception? At what points did individuals become personally involved? Why?

EXERCISE V. Fantasizing About Anxiety

Purpose: 1) To learn to use fantasy as a means of becoming aware of unconscious material.

2) To allow individuals to focus on their anxious feelings and reactions to those feelings.

Directions:

1) The setting should be relaxed and free. If possible, participants could lie on the floor. If there is not room for this, ask participants to sit in a relaxed posture and to close their eyes. Take about three minutes for persons to unwind. Ask them to try to free their minds of all thought. They might try to imagine a blank white screen. Indicate that as you begin talking you would like for them to take an imaginary trip. Talk slowly, pausing between sentences so that people will be able to imaginatively enter into the fantasy. (You may create your own fantasy according to what you think will arouse anxiety in your group.)

A Possible Fantasy. It is twilight, and you are in the middle of a strange, thick forest. You are following a narrow path, but it becomes less and less obvious. Parts of it are covered with leaves and broken limbs from trees. A light breeze arises and rustles through the trees. As you walk along, you are aware that it is getting darker and darker. The moon is not yet visible. How do you feel right now? You hear sounds of different forest animals running through the underbrush. How do you feel about those sounds? Can you smell anything? The prolonged slithering sound of slow movement along the ground assures you of the presence of a snake. Your walk hastens into a slow run as you gradually allow yourself to realize that indeed you are lost. You are hopelessly entangled in a forest you do not know. As you move on into the forest, what do you do now?

Allow two or three minutes for participants to finish the fantasy. You can judge time by completing your own.

2) Ask all who would like to share their fantasies to do so. Then explore whether through the fantasies anyone rediscovered or discovered (1) how he felt in anxiety-producing situations, and (2) how he reacted to anxiety. Did anyone notice any physical reactions? other reactions? How is each person feeling right now? How does the group feel about the fantasizing process?

If individuals were not able to really enter the fantasy, you could help them to explore that fact. In any event, allow plenty of time for participants to talk through the impact of the situation, regardless of what that impact was. Participants can grow in awareness of themselves and others as they share what actually happened.

Assignment

Ask participants to study chapter 5 in the participant's book.

Session
6

Purpose: To provide opportunity for persons
1) to share with others an experience in which they confronted anxiety in a constructive manner;
2) to explore strengths they have for confronting anxiety;
3) to become aware of potentialities and capacities they would like to develop.

EXERCISE I. Anxiety and Courage

Purpose: To share and understand better an experience in which the person moved out into some unknown area, risked standing on his own feet, and thereby used his capacity for being co-creator of his life.

Directions:

1) Divide the participants into trios, indicating that each member of the trio will take turns sharing an experience in which he felt personal growth occurred as he let go of the familiar and secure and stepped out into the new and unknown. Indicate that the experience related does not have to be a crucial, total life-changing event; it can be a small decision made in everyday life that called for courage to move forward. As each person in the trio relates such an experience, one listener should look for strengths he sees in the person which freed him to take this step into the unfamiliar. The second listener should try to really empathize with the speaker, attempting to feel how the person felt

(a) as he took the step; (b) after he accomplished the step; and (c) as he reflects on the event. Have these different functions for group members written on the board or newsprint so that each person can be clear about his task.

2) Tell trios to decide who will do what first, etc., and that you will call time for three rounds in the following manner: three minutes for sharing an experience and five minutes for listeners to report their observations and to check with the speaker.

3) Ask trios to summarize any findings they have made about personal growth. Allow ten minutes for this discussion.

4) Bring the entire group back together to share their findings. Then explore the following statement:

> Any growth toward becoming fully human involves overcoming anxiety by the exercise of personal courage.

What is the statement saying? Why do you agree or disagree with it?

EXERCISE II. The Courage to Risk Becoming
(intellectually demanding)

Purpose: 1) To examine the constructive use of normal anxiety.

2) To explore with others one's potentialities for facing anxiety constructively.

Directions:

1) Divide the participants into groups of six. Read the following quotation slowly and have the related paragraphs and questions below it duplicated for individual study.

> It is in intentionality and will that the human being experiences his identity. "I" is the "I" of "I can." Descartes was wrong in his famous sentence, "I think, therefore, I am," for identity does not come out of thinking as such, and certainly not out of intellectualization. Des-

cartes's formulation leaves out . . . exactly the variable that is most significant; it jumps from thought to identity, when what actually occurs is the intermediate variable of "I can." Kierkegaard mocked Hegel's similarly oversimplified and intellectualistic solution that "potentiality goes over into actuality" when he proclaimed that potentiality does go into actuality, *but the intermediate variable is anxiety.* We could rephrase it, "potentiality is experienced as *mine*—my power, my question—and, therefore, whether it goes over into actuality depends to some extent on me—where I throw my weight, how much I hesitate," and so on. What happens in human experience is "I conceive—I can—I will—I am." The "I can" and "I will" are the essential experiences of identity. This saves us from the untenable position in therapy of assuming that the patient develops a sense of identity and *then* acts. On the contrary, he experiences the identity *in* the action, or at least in the possibility for it.

. . . Normal, constructive anxiety goes with becoming aware of and assuming one's potentialities. Intentionality is the constructive use of normal anxiety. If I can have some expectations and possibility of acting on my powers, I move ahead. But if the anxiety becomes overwhelming, then the possibilities for action are blotted out.[1]

The way you react to normal anxiety converts that anxiety either into an immobilizing force destroying awareness of your vitality and power, or into a creative stimulus empowering you to act and grow—to co-create yourself. If you are able to confront anxiety, to incorporate it within yourself, anxiety becomes a force for self-realization.

The courage to take this kind of risk can come as you are able to face and accept the inescapable uncertainties of finite existence. This kind of acceptance arises within a relationship of faith and trust in the ultimate core of reality as being basically *for* man, not hostile to man. Faith and trust grow as man takes part in the self-affirmation of being which overcomes and prevails against nonbeing. In faith, as man acts in spite of anxiety and threat, he thereby expresses the courage to participate in that being. He expresses the courage to be and he gains greater courage to become.

Consider these questions: What exactly is the source of normal anxiety in your own experience? What powers do you have within yourself to act in spite of the threats anxiety brings? What gives you the courage to put those powers into action? How do you feel when and after you have acted on such courage?

Instruct the groups to take about twenty minutes to study the statements individually and then to discuss them by answering the questions in the last paragraph.

2) After twenty minutes (or less if participants seem bogged down in theoretical discussion), ask each participant to share with the other five in his group the following (have these printed on the board):

a) The thing about life which is most threatening to me.

b) How I live with that particular threat.

After individual sharing, if any person feels he ought to be able to confront his threat in a more constructive manner, other members in the group should tell the sharer any strengths or potentialities they observe within him which might enable him to live more creatively with the threat indicated.

EXERCISE III. Fantasizing

If you did not use the fantasy exercise (No. V) in the last session, think through its possibilities for this session. If you do use it during this session, focus particularly on (1) fantasies in which individuals faced an anxiety-producing situation constructively, and (2) potentialities and strengths of the individuals which were called into action in the fantasy.

EXERCISE IV. Overcoming Anxiety

Purpose: To explore strengths individuals have for confronting a situation they see as anxiety-producing.

Directions:

1) Divide the participants into groups of four. Ask each group to create and put on paper a specific, detailed description of a situation in which they think the average person would experience normal anxiety.

2) Ask groups to exchange descriptions so that each group has one not written by his group.

3) The new description should be read in each subgroup and each of the four should tell (a) how he would react in the situation as he identifies with one of the persons in the situation, and (b) what strengths he thinks he has that would allow him to react in this manner. After each has shared his feelings about himself and his reactions, other members should indicate any additional strengths they see in the sharer which might be used in the situation described.

Assignment

Ask class members to read chapter 6.

Session
7

Purpose: To provide opportunity for persons to grow in self-awareness of
1) personal limitations;
2) personal strengths and powers;
3) how each uses his freedom to be a co-creator of his life;
4) how each fears use of his freedom and allows outside forces to determine his life.

EXERCISE I. Freedom—Fear—Anxiety

Purpose: To provide a setting in which persons can explore with others the relationship of fear, anxiety, and freedom as they express themselves in the lives of individual participants.

Directions:

1) Before the class session, make arrangements to have the dialogue beginning on page 157 of the resource section read by two good readers.

2) Distribute pencils and paper and ask each person to take ten to fifteen minutes to write his own dialogue with fear. Note that Keen is using the term "fear" to mean the experience that May calls "anxiety." In the dialogue, persons might want to express things such as (a) ways they see anxiety affecting their own lives—positive and negative aspects; (b) ways they see their need for safety, security, and comfort affecting their desire for

greater freedom and self-determination; and (c) the relationship they see between anxiety, growth, and freedom. Indicate that their major concern should be to examine their own experience, not to write an impressive paper.

3) Instruct each participant to pair up with another to share and discuss what they have seen about themselves by either reading their dialogue or stating its major content.

4) About ten to fifteen minutes before the close of the session, call the total group back together and ask them, reflecting upon what they have just shared, to evaluate Keen's statement: "Decision is the alternative to fear. I can take upon myself the responsibility for deciding, and then the pain of limitation is not imposed but chosen. Maturity rather than fate or fear may determine the shape my life will assume."

EXERCISE II. Strength Bombardment

Purpose: 1) To share with others strengths one experiences in oneself.

2) To hear others express strengths they experience in the sharer.

Directions:

1) Each person takes a turn in which he:
   a) spends about three minutes sharing with the group the strengths he experiences in himself;
   b) listens to other members of the group suggest strengths they see in him.

2) After each person who wants to has taken his turn, individuals should contribute their impressions of what happened, how they felt as they told others of their strengths and as they heard others talk about their strengths.

EXERCISE III. Road of Life

Purpose: To take an overview of one's life and to reflect on this overview with another to determine
1) which events reveal self-determination;
2) which events reveal lack of self-determination.

Directions:

1) Distribute pencils and paper (or large index cards) to all participants. Each person is to put a dot on his paper to represent his birth. Then, without lifting his pencil from the paper, he is to portray, in any fashion he chooses, the series of critical incidents which he feels are representational of his life. Allow five to ten minutes.

2) Ask participants to pair off and to explain their illustration to their partner. The pair should then try to decide whether the person was exercising his freedom and power of self-determination in each crucial incident portrayed or whether he was allowing outside forces to determine the shape and direction of his life.

3) Ask pairs to join with other pairs in groups no larger than ten persons each. In the larger group they should share any findings they have made about life creation and (a) the role of self-determination; (b) the role of outside influences; and (c) the relationship of the two.

A Variation. Have each participant divide a piece of paper into twelve sections. In each section each person illustrates, in comic-strip fashion, an experience which he sees as formative in his life. Then proceed with steps 2 and 3.

EXERCISE IV. Choosing One's Self

Purpose: To grow in awareness of self and how one exercises his freedom.

1) Read and discuss with class members the paragraphs on pages 95–96 of the participant's book. Begin with "The basic

step . . ." and read that paragraph and the next two. Questions such as the following might be helpful in the discussion:

How does one "choose one's self"? What is chosen? What limitations have to be chosen? What possibilities have to be chosen? Can you think of a time when you chose yourself? Did your feeling toward responsibility change? How? Did your feeling toward discipline change? Is the thought conveyed in the three paragraphs basically a selfish, self-centered approach to life? Explain. Does it suggest we shouldn't receive help from others in life decisions? Explain.

2) Ask participants to pair off and to share how each would complete the following statements. Remind the group that anyone is free to withhold completions if he so desires. You might also want to remind them that all information shared is confidential. You will need to have copies of the sentences below.

The thing I find easiest to accept in myself is . . .
The thing I find hardest to accept in myself is . . .
I find it hard to accept responsibility for myself
   in the following areas:
I rebel against responsibility when . . .
I find it easy to accept responsibility when . . .
The hardest decision I ever had to make was . . .
I made the decision by . . .
After making it I felt . . .
I feel I am able to discipline myself when . . .
I feel most free when . . .
I could be more free if . . .

During this period of self-disclosure, partners should seek to really listen to each other—to be *present for* the other.

Assignment

Ask participants to continue their work on "Suggestions for Thought and Action," chapters 5 and 6.

Session

8

Purpose: To provide an opportunity for individuals
1) to explore their deep feelings and needs;
2) to discover relationships these feelings and needs may have for meanings they find in life.

EXERCISE I. Perception, Thought, Feeling (somewhat sophisticated)

Purpose: 1) To help participants make sharp distinctions between perceptions, thoughts, and feelings.
2) To learn to relate feeling feedback to observable behavior.
3) To practice empathizing with others.

Directions:

1) Divide participants into groups of four or five. Then state the purpose of the exercise and interpret what will be happening in the four rounds described below.

The following should be written on the board in view of all:

Round 1—Now I see . . .
Round 2—Now I think . . .
Round 3—Now I feel . . .
Round 4—Now I think you feel . . .

2) Indicate that in round 1, participants are to describe any nonverbal behavior of other members of their group by statements which begin with the phrase "Now I see." Illustrate by describing

some nonverbal behavior you observe in one of the class members. Ask groups to begin and call time after three to five minutes.

3) In round 2 participants should be asked to begin each statement with "Now I think." Illustrate with some thought which is running through your mind as you talk. Call time after five minutes.

4) Statements in round 3 should begin with "Now I feel."

After about three to five minutes of group interaction, interrupt and indicate that persons often tend to center their attention on the other person rather than express their own feelings. Another tendency is to confuse feelings and thoughts. Ask groups to take three minutes to check to see if they have observed either of these two tendencies in their interaction.

Now tell them to continue for five more minutes, being more aware of communicating just feelings. Suggest that they avoid qualifying phrases such as "I feel like . . ." and "I feel that . . ." In the remainder of this round they should simply use the phrase "I feel . . ."

5) In round 4 tell participants to strive to practice empathetic understanding of each other as they exchange feedback based on observable behavior. Observations should begin with "Now I think you feel . . ." and members should engage in dialogue to check the accuracy of their perceptions of other's feelings. Allow ten minutes for this round.

6) Call the groups together to discuss what actually happened. Did members have difficulty distinguishing feelings from thoughts? If so, why do they think this occurred? Did the experience indicate that individuals are not "in touch" with their feelings? If so, what would help us to be more aware of our feelings? Can we know that we really want anything if we are not in touch with our feelings? Why? Were group members able to pick up feelings of others? Did anyone find that his nonverbal communication

conveyed a message which was misrepresenting his feelings? What does that tell us? How can we express more fully what we are feeling? Can we fully respond to another person if we do not know what he is feeling at the time? You will need to gear all these questions to what participants actually experienced during the exercise.

EXERCISE II. Feelings and Communication Through
            Physical Expression (high risk)

Purpose: 1) To accept our physical body as part of God's gift to our total selves.
            2) To use physical expression to communicate with each other.
            3) To explore the relationship of our bodies to feelings.
            4) To explore those feelings which arise as participants are involved in experiences that relate to our needs for inclusion, freedom, and affection.

Directions:

1) Inclusion. In groups of six to eight, members form a tight circle, and one at a time each member steps outside the circle and has to try to break into the "in group." Instruct members that they can exert as much force (without violence) as necessary.

Ask members to share their feelings about what they just did. How did they feel as they tried to break in? to keep someone out? Are these feelings related to prior experiences of acceptance and rejection?

2) Freedom. Group members continue standing in a circle, and one at a time each individual goes into the center of the circle. He is asked to deal with the circle of people as a problem that stands between him and his freedom. The person in the center is to break out of the circle. Other group members are to do

everything they can to keep the person in the circle. After everyone has done this, group members discuss what has happened and how they felt about it.

3) Affection. Again, group members form a circle. Persons go one at a time to the center of the circle and close their eyes. Other group members go, one at a time, to the person in the center and nonverbally express the positive feelings they have toward him. The person in the center is to receive this expression without returning it—to experience receiving without giving back.

At the end members discuss what happened and how they felt about it. What were the different reactions to and feelings about giving to another and receiving from another? Did anyone feel he was unable really to express what he felt toward another? Why? What ways can we relate this experience to giving and receiving affection in everyday life?

4) Bring all groups together and share general reactions to the total group experience. How do members feel about what just occurred? Why? Was this a difficult experience for individuals? Why? Did individuals find it easier to communicate positive or negative feelings? Why? Have individuals discovered anything about physical expression of their feelings? What connection do they find between their bodies and their feelings? [1]

EXERCISE III. Alter Ego

Purpose: 1) To bring out some of the motives and feelings which one does not recognize or hopes to conceal.

2) To test one's ability to sense feelings not overtly expressed.

3) To learn a technique for increasing empathy and understanding of hidden factors in individuals and groups.

Directions:

1) Have participants seated in circles of up to ten each. Explain that you will start a discussion and that during the discussion any person may become an "alter ego" (other self) for another when he thinks that the other person is really feeling or meaning something which he is not saying clearly. The alter ego will speak up for that person with what he thinks has been left unsaid. When any person wants to become an alter ego, he should get up and stand for a time behind the chair of the person he wishes to represent. He then speaks as the alter ego. Indicate that no more than two alter egos should operate at one time. To have more becomes confusing.

2) Initiate a discussion within each circle on "The Thing I Value Most in Life." Do not try to direct the discussion or keep it on the subject. Simply let it proceed. As soon as some member feels that another person is not conveying some significant feeling, interpretation, or idea, he should become that person's alter ego.

3) A few minutes after alter egos have arisen and spoken for others, stop the discussion and let alter egos return to their places. Review in the group what happened, how the group felt about the offerings of the alter egos, how the persons who had alter egos felt about the offerings, etc.

4) Start the discussion again and continue until all who want the experience of having or being an alter ego have had this opportunity.

5) A few minutes before the end of your time together, discuss with the entire group what happened. Did persons come into closer touch with what they were feeling through their alter egos? Did anyone learn anything about his ability to communicate clearly? about his lack of perception of other's feelings? about his need to conceal feelings or thoughts? What did he learn? What was learned about the self? others? group interaction?[2]

EXERCISE IV. Feelings—Needs—Values

Purpose: To allow participants to

1) identify and share with others their deepest "felt needs";

2) to explore with others possible relationships between needs and values.

Directions:

1) Spend five to ten minutes giving participants time to unwind, pull apart from their everyday life, and turn inward. You could ask the group simply to close their eyes, sit in a relaxed position, and try to get in touch with themselves. Or you might use as a group activity one of the relaxation exercises suggested on pages 102–103 of the student's book.

2) Now ask group members, still with eyes closed, to spend a short time in self-conscious contemplation, trying to identify one "felt need" which they believe is the most important need they have at this particular time in their lives. After three to five minutes, ask members to see how they *feel* about themselves as they consider their need.

3) Instruct persons to form groups of three to share their deepest felt needs and the feelings they have about them. Small group members should be free to question each other for clarification of what is said or to contribute feelings they think may be going on in the person but are unexpressed.

4) After five to ten minutes ask group members to finish this part of the process and move on to have each person, in a few minutes of self-conscious examination, try to identify several things (persons, experience, quality of life, etc.) he values most in life. Group members should then (a) share the values they identified, and (b) see if the three together can see any relationship between the felt need and the values identified by each. Does

the need relate to some value? Does the need conflict with values held? Do individual needs tend to create values? Or do values and needs simply exist together with no relationship?

5) About ten minutes before the close of the session, call the large group together to contribute any findings they have about feelings, needs, and values, and their relationship as they are expressed in individual lives.

Assignment

Ask participants to read chapter 7. If you plan to use Exercise IV of session 9, ask the group to bring old magazines or ads to the next class session.

Session

9

Purpose: To help persons
    1) become more aware of values operating in their lives as motivating factors;
    2) examine how these values were developed;
    3) hear others speak about their values and how these values were formed. .

EXERCISE I. Cultivating an Awareness of Values

Purpose: To involve persons in a process through which they can
    1) become more aware of and identify values that are operating in their lives (motivating their actions);
    2) clarify how important these values are for them;
    3) explore possible ways these values were developed;
    4) identify values which may be held intellectually but which do not in reality motivate their decisions and actions;
    5) experience how others may influence one's values within a social setting.

Directions:

1) Divide the participants into several groups of six to eight persons. See that each person has paper and pencil. Then give each group a set of the following items (if this is not possible a list will suffice): a dollar bill; TV guide or movie guide (clipped from newspaper); an aspirin; a toy gun; car keys; a textbook, dictionary, or encyclopedia; a Bible; a valentine; a copy of the

Bill of Rights or the Declaration of Independence; a picture of a house or house keys.

2) Instruct each group to come to an agreement as to what value each of the objects above will symbolize for them. For example, aspirin may symbolize good health, medical care, a cop-out or escape from difficult things in life, man's control over nature. The dollar bill may symbolize money, material possessions, getting ahead in one's profession, freedom from material needs, or security. The gun might symbolize power, self-defense and security, aggression. Give several examples so the group will understand their task.

3) After each group has decided what each object symbolizes in terms of possible values, each individual is to make a list in which he arranges the objects in order according to their importance for him (i.e., according to his own hierarchy of values).

4) Next, each group should come to an agreement as to how these objects are to be ordered. That is, they should make a list indicating how the group as a whole rates the importance of each value symbolized. This requires that each individual mention his own ordering and why he followed it.

When several groups are involved, each group can present its list to the entire group for comparison, of both the interpretation of the symbols and the ordering of the values they represent. It would be interesting to see if any consensus emerges. There is a great deal of learning that can take place in the groups as you discuss interpretations of symbols and the hierarchies of values, so ample time should be provided for this phase of the exercise.

5) When all comparing is completed, lead the entire group in discussion by using questions similar to the following:

    a) Did you have difficulty in deciding on what value each object would symbolize? Why?

    b) How did you feel when you realized that you were not always in agreement with others? Did you want to

convince them of your interpretation, or were you
eager to agree with them? Does this tell you anything
about yourself? Could you agree with the group's final
decision?

c) Did you have difficulty in ordering the objects? Why or
why not?

d) Did you find it difficult to come to a group agreement
on the ordering of the objects? Did you find yourself
backing down? Or did you seek to persuade others
of the correctness of your suggestions? What were
your feelings about yourself and others during this
process?

e) Do you think there are some values important to you
that are left out in your ordering of objects? What are
they?

f) Do you think your final group ordering of objects would
be acceptable to most people in the U.S.? to most
Christians? Are there groups in our society whom you
feel would disagree with your group's final ordering?
How do you feel about that? Do you think someone
from a different culture would decide on a different
ordering of the same list of values—for example, a
Russian or someone from an oriental culture? What
does your answer indicate?

g) Think about your individual list of values. How did
each value gain importance for you? From experience? rational thought? personal inner need? How?
How much do you think other persons influenced your
value formation—parents, church, friends, society at
large? How do you feel about factors or persons who
influenced your selection of life values?

h) Is your final ordering of values really acceptable to
you? Do you see any areas of conflict between values?
Was your value structure painful for you to recog-

nize? Are there changes you would like to make? How can they occur?

i) Do you think you will naturally change these values as you grow older? Why or why not? Are there values you think you will never change? Why?

6) At the end of the session allow a few minutes for individuals to pull together discoveries they have made about themselves.[1]

NOTE: This exercise offers the possibility of a lengthy session. If you do not have a long period of time and if you feel it will be worthwhile, you may want to continue discussion of the session in your next group meeting, even though something will be lost with the passage of time.

EXERCISE II. A Variation

You could easily create a group experience centered on the concerns listed in No. 2 of "Action Learning" on page 118 of the student's text. Group members could discuss these concerns in groups of three or four, and then the larger group could share findings through questions similar to those used in Exercise I of this session.

EXERCISE III. Meaning and Motivation

Purpose: To provide a period of time for self-examination and self disclosure through which participants may become more aware of

    1) aspects of life which have value for them;

    2) motivational factors operating in their lives.

Directions:

1) Ask participants to pair off for a period of self-examination, self-disclosure, and exploration of motivational factors operating in their individual lives.

2) See that each person has paper and pencil and a copy of the incomplete sentences below:

Set I

I am happiest when . . .

I am most alive when . . .

The thing that turns me on most is . . .

The most meaningful thing in life is . . .

I think I would give up my life for . . .

My acts show that what I care most about in life is . . .

Set II

I am most unhappy when . . .

I am nearly always depressed when . . .

The thing that turns me off most is . . .

The least meaningful activity I engage in is . . .

The factor I observe which seems most destructive to persons is . . .

The thing I care about the least in life is . . .

3) Instruct each person to ask his partner to complete the sentences in Sets I and II, jotting down the central content of each answer for his partner. Indicate that in answering the questions first associations are often more honest than well-thought-out and "filtered" answers. Allow five to ten minutes for each person in the pair to answer questions.

4) After each partner has answered the questions, instruct each person to examine the answers he has given against the following questions. (Have these questions duplicated or posted for all to view.)

Questions related to Set I:

Do you see yourself moving toward the experiences, relationships, and activities you talked about in your answers to Set I? If not, why not? If you actively sought these experiences, would you feel that you were being selfish?

Why? What do your answers to the first group of questions indicate about what you value most in life? List these values. How do you see these values operating in your life as motivational forces? Do they motivate most of your decisions and acts? many of them? few of them?

Questions related to Set II:

As you reflect on your life, are you very much involved in many of the experiences, relationships, and acts you described in your answers? If your answer is yes, why? In looking at your listing of negative aspects of life, try to determine exactly why each one is destructive to you or to human life in general. Through a process of looking at opposites, try to determine if any positive life values are suggested which you had not included in your answers to Set I.

5) After this period of self-examination, ask partners to share their findings with each other. Indicate that this sharing should not just include specific answers to questions but also any discoveries the person has made about himself and the motivational factors in his life.

6) Call the entire group together. Close the session by asking participants to share what they have seen as valuable in human life. List these on the board.

EXERCISE IV. Society and Values

Purpose: To provide an experience through which persons can
1) identify values which they think are held by most persons in our society;
2) become aware of how these values affect their own lives.

Directions:

1) Have a large number of magazines or ads from magazines available for use during the class session.

2) Involve the class in a brief discussion (two to five minutes) of the fact that much of modern advertising is based upon the selling of a product by appealing to some of the consumer's basic psychological drives, needs, and motivations—i.e., the consumer is made to think that a particular product will help fill some basic human need. Then ask all group members to thumb through ads to determine what each is suggesting as a value in life—something worth caring about and getting. (If time is available, provide paste, scissors, and sheets of newsprint, and ask participants to make a collage of pictures and words from ads to indicate what ad creators think the average person in the U.S. values and cares about in life. This activity would require more of the person's creative efforts and would therefore allow persons to become more involved in the task.)

3) Have the participants divide into smaller groups of four to six and instruct them to share their findings. Ask them to make a composite listing on newsprint of the ten values in life which they feel are the top motivators determining individual decisions and actions for people in the U.S. These values should be listed in order of importance.

4) Bring the entire group together and have each post its findings. If there is a great deal of variation in these listings, and if there is time, have the total group create its own value priority listing. A great deal of learning can take place as individuals discuss various values and interact with one another in an effort to come to agreement on a hierarchy of values.

5) Ask individuals to spend a few minutes in silence to reflect on how these values of society affect their own lives.

6) Involve the group in a period of sharing through questions similar to the following: Did you find that you accept and act on most of the values we have listed? Which ones do you see operating most often in your life? Which ones least often? Are there values you do not think are really important for human life? Which ones? Did you find other life values which are more important for you in motivating your own decisions and acts? What are they? Do you think society should influence what we care about in life? Why? How much? As you examined your own life, did you discover any factors that motivate your own life which you would like to change? If so, how can such change occur? Were there areas in which you wished society did not influence you so much? What were they? What can you do about influences you do not like? Again, questions must be geared to actual findings of your group.

Assignment

Have the group study chapter 8 over to "The Role of the Conscience in the Mature Person," pages 121–131. If you plan to use Exercise I or II of the next session, make plans for the role play with class members. Exercise III may require asking others to help you assemble materials.

Session
10

Purpose: To provide an experience through which persons can
  1) examine their valuing, the process through which they make decisions;
  2) become more aware of factors (conscience, laws, introjected values, conceived values, personal needs and goals) which may influence their decisions and acts.

EXERCISE I. Decision-Making

Purpose: Identical with those listed for the session as a whole. In addition, this exercise will allow persons to generalize about factors which may help them move toward more responsible decision-making.

Directions:

1) Have the following problem situation (or another you or the group creates) presented by role play or by telling it. Of course, the role play would make the problem more lifelike. (See directions for role play on page 50.)

Situation. You are the professional director of a neighborhood center in an underprivileged area of your city. For the past few months a twenty-year-old man, James, has been working with you in an afternoon tutoring program for young teen-agers. You are impressed with him as a person and he has done very good work, especially with Kerry, a tenth grader who has become quite attached to James. Kerry lives with his mother and two older sisters, and as far as you know, there is no strong male image in his life. You see the relationship with James as very beneficial to Kerry's growth.

A parole officer makes a visit to you to ask about James' involvement with youth through your center. He indicates that James has a record. He was imprisoned for a two-year period on a burglary conviction. During the trial, suspicion of his using and selling drugs arose but was never proved. You feel you have a responsibility to James, Kerry, Kerry's family, and for the work of the center. What will you do?

2) Divide the participants into groups of six, and ask each group quickly to allow each person to say as simply as possible what he would do as director of the center. He should make no explanation as to why he came to that decision.

3) Next, realizing that our quick first reactions often reflect much of what we really feel and value in life, ask participants to move behind their initial decision to see what factor or factors may have influenced the decision—an introjected value? a moral law or rule? concern for a person? a personal need or fear? a deeply held personal value? conscience? a prejudice? What?

4) After a few minutes for private searching, each person should tell his small group, as briefly as possible, the factors he identified as influencing his decision.

5) Instruct each small group to become the Board of Directors of the center and to decide what should be done about James and his involvement in the work of the center. Allow fifteen minutes for this process.

6) After the group has arrived at a decision, ask them to (a) analyze the group's decision-making process—how did they come to their decision? what steps did they take?—and (b) evaluate the group process. Was it a helpful process? What was good about it? Were there steps taken which hindered responsible decision-making? What were they? Allow fifteen minutes for this.

7) If time allows, ask a representative from each "Board" to report its decision. This would be helpful, as it would reveal the

many possibilities that are open to us in decision-making. Often our freedom is limited by lack of vision concerning possibilities available to us. If your time is limited, move on to step 8, omitting this step.

8) Involve the entire group in outlining factors they think are important for responsible group decision-making. Look at this listing to see if the group thinks the decision-making process they have designed could be used for individual decision-making. Why or why not?

EXERCISE II. The Function of the Conscience

Purpose: To allow persons
          1) to become aware of various roles and functions of the conscience as it operates in individual lives;
          2) to evaluate those roles and functions.

Directions:

1) Through role play present the problem situation suggested in Exercise I or select a problem situation which may be more involving for your particular group.

2) As soon as the problem has been clearly defined through role play, cut the action and shift to a second scene—the meeting of the Director with the center's Board (three persons). Ask for four persons to volunteer for the required roles and a fifth to serve as the conscience of the Director. Allow a few minutes to give participants time to identify with their roles. Instruct the conscience to stand behind the Director's chair and to tell him anything he feels is appropriate as the discussion proceeds. Board members and the Director should actively strive to come to a decision about James and his work with the center. Instruct the class members who will be observing that if anyone feels the conscience is not saying what he should, the observer can exchange places with him. (This process of changing the conscience can

continue on a volunteer basis, or you may want to stop the role play at particular points to ask for a new conscience.)

3) After ten to fifteen minutes of role play, cut the action and analyze what happened. What different functions of the conscience were observed? Were there times when the conscience hindered responsible decision-making? helped the Director move toward being more responsible? How did the Director feel about the various roles of the conscience? Can he see ways in which the conscience might have played a more creative role?

After looking at how different members of the class viewed the work of the conscience through the role play, ask class members if there are additional ways they see their consciences influencing their lives. Then move into a general analysis of the function of the conscience by using questions similar to those in step 5 of the next exercise.

EXERCISE III. My Conscience

Purpose: To allow group members to

1) become more aware of the role of their conscience in their lives;

2) evaluate the role their conscience plays in responsible decision-making.

Directions:

1) Have newsprint or posterboard, old magazines, newspapers, crayons or other drawing equipment, paste, and scissors on hand.

2) Ask participants to create a collage or draw two different representations on his newsprint. On the left half, each is in some way to make a representation of how he experiences his conscience. On the right half, each in some way should indicate how his conscience generally makes him feel. Allow twenty minutes for this part of the exercise.

3) Ask members to pair off and to share with each other their

pictures or collages and the meaning they have. Allow five to ten minutes.

4) (If there is time, move through both steps 4 and 5. If your time is limited, choose the process that you think would be most beneficial for your group.) In the entire group have those who would like to to share their creations. Some persons might like to have their partners tell about their representations. This might be a good way to test listening abilities and for individuals to gain further insights into their own creation.

5) Involve the entire group in a discussion of the role of the conscience in growth toward becoming a mature, free but responsible person. The discussion could be initiated by asking: What is the function of the conscience? How can it help you become a mature, free but responsible person? How do you think society, the family, and the church influence the formation of the conscience? How responsible is an individual for his own conscience formation? Can you think of times when your conscience has helped you in growth toward maturity? has hindered growth toward maturity? If you could change the way your conscience operates in your life, what changes would you make?

Assignment

Ask participants to study the final section of chapter 8. The two exercises in the next session will require that the Self-Appraisal Inventory found on page 108 be mimeographed and distributed at the end of this session. Ask participants to complete the inventory and bring it to the next class session.

Session
11

Purpose: To allow group members to
   1) in a period of self-disclosure confess their need for change;
   2) hear God's healing word of accepting, forgiving love spoken through the Scriptures;
   3) feel God's healing word active through the community of the Holy Spirit.

EXERCISE I. Self-Inventory—Disclosure—Acceptance

NOTE: If there is the possibility that you could have an extended period of time for this session or two meetings to deal with this area, it would be very helpful to use Exercise II in conjunction with and prior to this exercise.

Purpose: Identical with the session purpose.

Directions:

1) Participants should have brought with them the completed Self-Appraisal Inventory which was distributed in the preceding session.

2) Ask the group to pair off and to take five to ten minutes to share the five things about themselves they would most like to change. In sharing, each should include his feelings about the areas of needed change, and the listener should feel free to contribute his impression of what is being said.

3) Ask participants to form groups of six by joining three pairs together. In these groups, each person should state *for his partner* the areas of needed and desired change of the partner. Allow about ten minutes for this exchange.

4) With persons sitting in groups of six, read or have several persons read the Scripture passages listed below. Make arrangements for this before the session and be certain each person knows the order in which the passages are to be read. They can read the Scripture where they are seated. Before the readings, ask participants to seek to allow God's Word to speak to them personally. After the readings, pause for a few minutes of silence to allow this to happen.

> Luke 5:30–32; Luke 7:36–50; John 13:3–15; Luke 22:27; Mark 9:36–37; John 14:15–17.

5) Now ask participants to take turns standing in the center of their circle. Other members who would like to should seek to express to that person in any nonverbal manner which seems appropriate God's healing-forgiving-accepting love for that person.

If you think your class does not feel free enough with each other to express nonverbally their loving concern for and support of each other, you could use the following variation. After the reading and silence, ask the small groups to share what they felt about themselves, others, and God's forgiving love as the passages were read.

6) Close the session by reading 1 Peter 2:21–25.

SELF-APPRAISAL INVENTORY

Name ———————————————————— Date ——————————

Col. B Total ——————————————————————————————

(Fill in after completion of test.)

Purpose: This inventory is designed to help you get a realistic picture of your true feelings about yourself. The only "right" answer is that which you feel genuinely describes you as you really are now. Do not pretend to be either better or worse. Try to discard any mask or blinders. The only purpose is to help you in your own development.

Directions:

Read each item and decide how truly it describes you. Answer by placing in the blanks in *Column A* in front of each number:

+ + if it is *very true* of you; *very much like* you.

  + if it is more *like* than unlike you.

  O if you can't decided; 50–50.

  − if it is more *unlike* you than like you.

− − if it is *quite untrue* of you; *very much unlike* you; *just the opposite* of what you are.

Rate Here Col. A (As I now am)	Col. B (Desire to change)	*Item No.*	*Descriptive Item* (How true is this of you?)
———	———	1.	I have a horror of failure in anything I want to accomplish.
———	———	2.	I am contented.
———	———	3.	I am no one. Nothing seems to be me.
———	———	4.	I am relaxed and nothing really bothers me.
———	———	5.	I usually like people.
———	———	6.	I see myself as having something to give to others.
———	———	7.	I am a responsible person.
———	———	8.	I am aware of being somewhat at cross-purposes with myself.
———	———	9.	I feel emotionally mature.
———	———	10.	I often do things when I'm in one mood which don't make sense to me later.

Rate Here			
Col. A (As I now am)	Col. B (Desire to change)	Item No.	Descriptive Item (How true is this of you?)
———	———	11.	Sometimes I feel that the things I do are genuinely right for me; sometimes I don't.
———	———	12.	All you have to do is just insist with me, and I give in.
———	———	13.	I feel cut off from other people and I long for deeper relationships.
———	———	14.	If others don't appreciate me, I feel that they don't know a good thing when they see it.
———	———	15.	I have the feeling that I am just not facing things.
———	———	16.	I can stand up for myself.
———	———	17.	I feel as if I were several very different persons, each struggling against the others.
———	———	18.	I often feel helpless.
———	———	19.	I often kick myself for the things I do.
———	———	20.	I am optimistic.
———	———	21.	I have initiative.
———	———	22.	I am assertive.
———	———	23.	I express my emotions freely.
———	———	24.	My decisions are not my own.
———	———	25.	I often feel humiliated.
———	———	26.	It's pretty tough to be me.
———	———	27.	I am open and honest with others and myself.
———	———	28.	I feel worthless.
———	———	29.	I keep starting things I don't finish.
———	———	30.	I often don't know how I feel about things.
———	———	31.	I can usually make up my mind and stick to it.
———	———	32.	I am at ease in deep relationships with the opposite sex.
———	———	33.	I feel that I am using and developing most of my gifts, talents, and powers.
———	———	34.	I feel like a zombie, walking around in a dream or a daze.

Rate Here

Col. A (As I now am)	Col. B (Desire to change)	*Item No.*	*Descriptive Item* (How true is this of you?)
————	————	35.	I am sexually attractive.
————	————	36.	I feel apathetic.
————	————	37.	I have a healthy love of myself.
————	————	38.	I doubt my sexual powers.
————	————	39.	I tend to be on my guard with people who are somewhat friendlier than I had expected.
————	————	40.	I feel vaguely anxious nearly all the time.
————	————	41.	I am afraid of a full-fledged disagreement with a person.
————	————	42.	I usually feel driven.
————	————	43.	I feel guilty about every little thing.
————	————	44.	I often despise myself.
————	————	45.	I just can't get along with people.
————	————	46.	I can't seem to make up my mind one way or another.
————	————	47.	I understand myself.
————	————	48.	I have few values and standards of my own.
————	————	49.	I am impulsive.
————	————	50.	I feel hopeless and empty.
————	————	51.	I enjoy sex.
————	————	52.	I keep worrying about my health.
————	————	53.	It is difficult to control my aggression.
————	————	54.	I dislike my own sexuality.
————	————	55.	I feel comfortable in most situations.
————	————	56.	I find it easy to forgive myself.
————	————	57.	I seldom worry about anything once I've done it.
————	————	58.	I really enjoy life.
————	————	59.	I am dominated by "shoulds."
————	————	60.	I feel wholehearted in my actions and at one with myself.

Rate Here			
Col. A (As I now am)	Col. B (Desire to change)	*Item No.*	*Descriptive Item* (How true is this of you?)
———	———	61.	I have a warm emotional relationship with others.
———	———	62.	I don't really respect myself.
———	———	63.	I feel insecure within myself.
———	———	64.	I seldom put on a false front.
———	———	65.	I am easily hurt by others.
———	———	66.	I usually feel good about what I am doing.
———	———	67.	I am in touch with my feelings and I usually know what I want, care for, and value in life.
———	———	68.	I am self-reliant.
———	———	69.	I often find myself doing what I don't really want to do and neglecting what I think I want to do.
———	———	70.	I feel adequate.
———	———	71.	I am sensitive and responsive to other people.
———	———	72.	I find it easy to forgive others.

Further Directions:

1) Now read over each item again and decide whether, if you could, you would like to *change* in this particular characteristic. If you are fairly well satisfied to continue as you are with an item as answered in Column A, put a zero (0) in Column B.

If you'd like to change by having the item become *more true* of you than it now is, place a plus sign (+) in Column B.

If you'd like to change by having the item become *less true* of you than it now is, place a minus sign (−) in Column B.

2) when you have finished, count the total number of + and − items in Column B and enter it as "Column B Total" at the top of the first page of the inventory.

3) Finally, pick out the five items on which you now most *strongly want to change*. On these five, circle your Column A and B answers.[1]

EXERCISE II. Myself and Growth-Change

Purpose: 1) To identify and confess areas of personal dissatisfaction with self.

2) To explore with others possibilities of reducing emotional stress involved in growth-change.

Directions:

1) Have participants bring their completed Self-Appraisal Inventories to class.

2) With your entire group compare totals for Column B, as entered at the top of the first page.

3) Ask participants to form groups of four and to share with each other their feelings about the following questions. Have these posted for all to see.

HIGH TOTALS: Did you exaggerate your need for change? Were you overcritical of yourself?

LOW TOTALS: Are you too complacent with yourself? Have you given up? Have you been blind to some potential resources you have which if developed would bring fuller life?

Instruct groups that as each person shares his feelings about his total for Column B, other members of the group should express their feelings about that person's total as compared with the person as they experience him. They should be warned not to deny or try to change that person's perception of himself. Rather, they should simply state what they see and experience in the person.

4) With participants remaining in groups of four, ask each person (a) to look at the five items he has circled as areas in which he most desires change; (b) to decide on the one top priority for change; and (c) to share it with others in the group. As each person shares his top change priority, he and the group should try to decide (a) whether the change needed can occur as the individual begins to actualize potentials of his real self *in the present,*

or (b) whether it would be better to modify the change goal. In other words, what is possible for the person in the area seen as needing change? Is the person trying to actualize some idealized person? Is he playing a role? If so, attempted changes wouldn't really bring growth. Maybe the person needs to look at why he desires change in that area. Maybe graceful self-acceptance is needed. Perhaps acceptance of God's forgiving love may free the person from enslaving forces.

During this process, it may be helpful to remind participants of the section dealing with how change actually occurs through self-awareness, forgiveness, self-acceptance, and being one's true self. See pages 96 ff., "Growth in Self-Consciousness." Discussion should focus on helping each person grow in realistic understanding of himself and of the potentials of that real self which could be freed for changes he would like to see. The group should serve as a source of insight, forgiving love, and support for the person as he looks at himself.

EXERCISE III. Myself—Change—Forgiving-Accepting Love

Purpose: To provide opportunity for
1) self-examination and self-expression;
2) confession of need for change;
3) hearing God's healing word spoken through Scripture; and
4) feeling God's healing word active through the community of the Holy Spirit.

Directions:

1) Have collage and drawing materials available for use at the beginning of the session.

2) Instruct participants to place two representations on their newsprint or posterboard. On the left-hand side they should in some way represent their present understanding of themselves. On

the right-hand side they are to represent the person they would like to become. Allow twenty minutes. Ask participants to work in silence.

3) Have participants find a partner and share representations. During this time, about ten minutes, partners should communicate how they feel about what they have represented. The listener should feel free to dialogue with his partner about his impression of what is being said.

4) Ask pairs to join with two other pairs to form groups of six. In these groups each person is to show and tell about his partner's representation. Allow ten to fifteen minutes for this sharing.

5) Follow steps 4–6 of Exercise I for the closing of the session.

Assignment

All exercises suggested in the next (and last) session indicate the need for some duplicated material to be distributed at the close of this session, unless you can have at least two hours for the closing session.

Session
12

Purpose: To provide an experience through which participants can
1) pull together findings about themselves and their relationship to others, the world, and God;
2) come to a decision about some areas of growth each individual would like to nurture in himself as he (a) recognizes factors in present life involvement which may be hindering real self-growth, and (b) identifies aspects of the self which can be utilized for growth in the desired direction; and
3) become aware of the kinds of present life involvements which would strengthen the person for growth in the desired direction.

EXERCISE I. Fantasy

Purpose: Identical with the session purpose.

Directions:

This exercise will take at least a two-hour period of time. If you do not have a two-hour session, you could assign steps 1–3 to be done prior to the class session. Simply give persons instructions for the fantasy and a copy of the questions they should answer about their fantasy.

1) Ask participants to close their eyes, relax each part of their bodies, and let their minds become a blank. Then ask each to answer the following questions in his own mind. Pause after each question to give time for persons to form their answers.

Who are you—in your innermost core of selfhood?

As you look at things as they are for you today, what are the best aspects of your personal life?

When do you feel most fully alive?

What do you do really well?

What would you like to learn to do?

What would you like to do that you have never done before?

Now indicate that each person is to create a fantasy about his future and where he would like to be in terms of personal growth five years from now as the self he really is continues in growth. Indicate that you will begin the fantasy and allow time for each person to silently complete his own. Pause between sentences to allow imagination to begin its work.

Fantasy. After a good night's rest, you are waking up on a morning five years from now. What are your feelings as you awake? What are the first sounds and odors which come to your attention? What is the first sight which comes into vision? Think through the day ahead of you. What will you be doing today? What kind of person will you be?

Allow five to ten minutes for participants to complete their fantasy.

2) See that participants have paper and pencil. Ask them to jot down central features of their fantasy and then to do the following evaluation individually.

3) Evaluate your fantasy. Is this a realistic future for you?

A. If so, what parts of the fantasy should you be turning into reality now? What underdeveloped resources do you have which you can start using right now? What strengths do you now have which can be utilized as you move into your future? What weaknesses do you have which might prevent realization of your future becoming? What realistic limitations do you have which you will need to accept as you become your future? What kinds of present involvements will allow you to be the person you want to become?

B. If your fantasy does not seem to be a realistic future for you, try to answer the following: What is it that makes it difficult for me to accept my real self and my true potential? Is it some basic limitation of myself or my life situation? Am I trying to be some idealized self? Am I playing a role? What's behind this need for deception? What could free me from this need to deceive myself and others? How can I grow in awareness and acceptance of my real self? What kinds of experience can I open myself for?

4) Ask participants to take a moment to reflect on God's searching-judging-forgiving-healing love, which can become a reality in human dialogue.

5) Ask participants to pair off. If possible each person should select a person in the group with whom he would like to enter into a covenant relationship. This relationship would be one in which the persons contract with one another to provide support for each other as they continue to grow in self-knowledge and self-realization.

6) After participants have paired off, ask them to share their thoughts and feelings about their fantasies. During this time the listening partner should feel free to ask questions for clarification, to communicate his own interpretations and perceptions, and to evaluate the partner's understanding of his fantasy. Allow fifteen minutes for each person to share his fantasy and thoughts about it. Call time after the first fifteen minutes so that both partners will be able to share.

7) Call the entire group back together. Ask each person to spend a few minutes in silent contemplation of what has occurred within the group during the past weeks. Now ask each person to state the one thing he most hopes for in the life of his partner. Close by reading Hebrews 11:1–2; 12:1–2, 12, 15a; 13:1, 20–21.

EXERCISE II. A Variation

If you did not use Exercise III of session 11, it could be easily adapted for use in this session. Simply use the representations suggested in that exercise instead of the fantasy. Then adapt steps 2–4 of the exercise above.

EXERCISE III. Another Variation

Another variation which you could easily use in conjunction with the procedure indicated in Exercise I of this session is to have participants write their own obituary. The obituary should express the sorts of things they would like to be true of them at their death. If people have difficulty with creative writing, they could simply list words that they would like to have used to describe them. If you think an obituary sounds morbid, you could substitute a "Man (Woman) of the Year" newspaper article.

As you make a decision about which exercise you will use for this final section, you may uncover an idea of your own which will be more profitable for your particular group. What has happened among you? What do you need to do? Do you need to close with a study-discussion session? What?

Perhaps some groups may want to make plans for a continuation of their group life outside your regular study program. Others may want to begin new supportive, personal growth groups with additional persons. If you feel participants might be interested, explore the possibility with them.

Resource Section

Theory Papers

This section contains a variety of papers related to personal growth and group relationships. Some papers are included simply as additional information for group leaders. Others have been referred to in session plans, since they are directly related to particular exercises. Most of the papers could be used as basic information to be discussed in theory sessions (see pp. 24–25).

The Helping Relationship
and Feedback

I. Different names are used to designate the helping process, such as counseling, teaching, guiding, training, educating, leading. They have in common that the helping person is trying to influence (and therefore change) the individual who is being helped. The expectation is, furthermore, that the direction of the change in the receiver of help will be constructive and useful to him (i.e., it will clarify his perception of the problem, bolster his self-confidence, modify his behavior, develop new skills, etc.).

II. One way to look at the helping situation is to sketch it in the following manner:

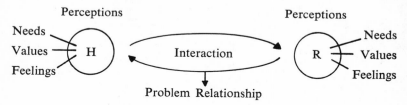

1. The helping situation is dynamic, i.e., characterized by interaction which is both verbal and nonverbal, and relationships.

2. The helping person has needs (biological and psychological), feelings, and a set of values.

This and the following six papers were adapted from *Theory and Skill,* developed by the Youth Office, Lutheran Church in America, Philadelphia.

3. The receiver of help has needs (biological and psychological), feelings, and a set of values.

4. Both helper and the receiver of help are trying to satisfy needs in the situation.

5. The helper has perceptions of himself, of the receiver of help, of the problem, and of the entire situation (experiences, roles, standards, etc.).

6. The receiver of help has perceptions of himself, of the helper, of the problem, and of the entire situation (experiences, roles, standards, etc.).

7. The interaction takes place in relation to some need or problem which may be external to the two individuals, interwoven with the relationship of the two individuals, or rooted in the relationship between the two individuals. Wherever the beginning point and the focus of emphasis, the relationship between the two individuals becomes an important element in the helping situation as soon as interaction begins.

8. His needs, values and feelings, and his perception of them as well as his perception of the situation (including the problem and the helper) cause the receiver of help to have certain objectives in the interaction which takes place.

III. To depict the helping situation as above suggests its complexity. It is not easy to give help to another individual in such a way that he will be strengthened to do a better job of handling his situation. Nor is it easy to receive help from another person—that is, the kind of help which makes us more adequate in dealing with our problems. If we really listen and reflect upon the situations in which we are either the helper or the receiver of help, we are not only impressed with the magnitude and range of the problems involved in the helping situation, but also realize that we can keep on learning as a helping person or a person receiving help as long as we live.

IV. Let us reflect on some of the things about us that make it difficult to *receive* help.

1. It is hard to really admit our difficulties even to ourselves. It may be even harder to admit them to someone else. There are concerns sometimes whether we can really trust the other person, particularly if it is in a work or other situation which might affect our standing. We may also be afraid of what the other person thinks of us.

2. We may have struggled so hard to make ourselves independent persons that the thought of depending on another individual seems to violate something within us. Or we may all our lives have looked for someone on whom to be dependent and we try to repeat this pattern in our relationship with the helping person.

3. We may be looking for sympathy and support rather than for help in seeing our difficulty more clearly. We ourselves may have to change as well as others in the situation. When the helper tries to point out some of the ways we are contributing to the problem, we may stop listening. Solving a problem may mean uncovering some of the sides of ourselves which we have avoided or wished to avoid thinking about.

4. We may feel our problem is so unique that no one could ever understand it and certainly not an outsider.

V. Let us reflect upon some of the things which make it difficult for us to *give* help.

1. Most of us like to give advice. Doing so suggests to us that we are competent and important. We easily get caught in a telling role without testing whether our advice is appropriate to the abilities, the fears, or the powers of the person we are trying to help.

2. If the person we are trying to help becomes defensive, we may try to argue or pressure him—meet resistance with more pressure and increase resistance. This is typical in argument.

3. We may confuse the relationship by only responding to one aspect of what we see in the other's problem and by over-

praising, avoiding recognition that the person being counseled must see his own role and his own limitations as well.

VI. To be fruitful the helping situation needs these characteristics:

1. Mutual trust.

2. Recognition that the helping situation is a joint exploration.

3. Listening, with the helper listening more than the individual receiving help.

VII. Because we are human, the potential for all the weaknesses and the strengths, the follies and the wisdom known to man exists at some level within us.

Human beings become more capable of dealing with their problems as success experiences give them a greater sense of adequacy to meet situations. This does not imply avoiding a recognition of the conflict issues and the inadequacies but means a recognition as well of the strengths and the success experiences.

VIII. Feedback is a way of helping another person to consider changing his behavior. It is communication to a person (or a group) which gives that person information about how he affects others. As in a guided missile system, feedback helps an individual keep his behavior "on target" and thus better achieve his goals.

Some criteria for useful feedback:

1. It is descriptive rather than evaluative. By describing one's own reaction, it leaves the individual free to use it or not as he sees fit. By avoiding evaluative language, it reduces the need for the individual to react defensively.

2. It is specific rather than general. To be told that one is "dominating" will probably not be as useful as to be told, "Just now when we were deciding the issue you did not listen to what others said and I felt forced to accept your arguments or face attack from you."

3. It takes into account the needs of both the receiver and the giver of feedback. Feedback can be destructive when it serves only our own needs and fails to consider the needs of the person on the receiving end.

4. It is directed toward behavior which the receiver can do something about. Frustration is only increased when a person is reminded of some shortcoming over which he has no control.

5. It is solicited, rather than imposed. Feedback is most useful when the receiver himself has formulated the kind of question which those observing him can answer.

6. It is well timed. In general, feedback is most useful at the earliest opportunity after the given behavior (depending, of course, on the person's readiness to hear it, support available from others, etc.).

7. It is checked to ensure clear communication. One way of doing this is to have the receiver try to rephrase the feedback he has received to see if it corresponds to what the sender had in mind.

8. When feedback is given in a training group, both giver and receiver have opportunity to check with others in the group the accuracy of the feedback. Is this one man's impression or an impression shared by others?

Feedback, then, is a way of giving help; it is a corrective mechanism for the individual who wants to learn how well his behavior matches his intentions; and it is a means of establishing one's identity for answering, "Who am I?"

Patterns of
Interpersonal Relationship

Objectives: To present and illustrate a theory of circular social process as applied to the analysis of interpersonal relations in a small group.

Let's start with two facts that are supported by studies of a wide variety of human groups:

1. When persons come together to form a group (children or adults), consensus develops very rapidly in the group as to who is liked a great deal and who is liked only a little; who is an expert and who isn't; who can get his own way and who can't. Everyone gets a position in the group on a number of hierarchies. This position is determined partly by what the member has done and does, and partly by the values and perceptions of the other members.

2. The second fact is that these hierarchies which are formed very rapidly tend to remain quite stable over time. The consensus of opinions and attitudes about each member tends to remain the same. His particular position in the group tends to remain stable in spite of the fact that many members may be making a variety of efforts to change their positions. Change of position in the group is feasible, but such change calls for careful diagnosis and special efforts. In the normal course of events the structure of interpersonal relations is quite stable and consistent from time to time and from activity to activity.

The object of this theory session is to present a theory that will help us understand why and how a member's relationship to the group does tend to get stabilized and to remain so, and the different patterns of relationship that develop.

We have called these concepts a "circular process" theory of interpersonal relations in the group. Let's look at the main features of the theory by reference to the diagram. Because this is a circular process, we could start at any point and follow the process around until it returns to the same point. Let's start with the upper left-hand corner and go around to get a quick overview. Then we'll return and look at the various elements in more detail.

A Quick Overview

The upper left-hand circle is labeled "Inner Processes Within the Member." Emerging from his feelings about himself and his attitudes toward others are intentions to act toward other people (line going to the right). These intentions, or some of them, become visible as behavior toward others (upper right-hand circle). We have called this the member's "behavior output," his social actions toward other members and toward the group as a whole. This behavior output is perceived by others and stimulates psychological processes within the other members (lower right-hand circle). These processes are the forming of expectations about how the member will behave and evaluations about him as a person and a member.

These expectations and evaluations result in intentions to behave in certain ways toward the member. Part of these intentions emerge as visible behavior toward the member ("Behavioral Feedback from Others," lower left-hand circle). Looking at it from the point of view of the particular member whose situation we are analyzing, we can think of the actions of other members toward him, or about him, as "behavioral input" which he can potentially perceive and use to get clues about how he is being reacted to by the other members. These perceptions activate another type of inner process within the member (upper left-hand corner), a process of trying to use the messages from others to reorient his attitudes and intentions ("processing feedback"). As you can readily see, this process keeps going on and on, many times in each meeting, for each member of the group.

An Example of Pattern of High Status and Acceptance in the Group

Let's look at the situation of *Member X.*

He accepts himself, sees himself as quite effective in relations with others, and has an attitude of friendly warmth toward others. His intentions, partly conscious and partly unconscious, are to express his ideas freely, to find out what other people are interested in, and to cooperate in group activities. His behavior output is active, friendly, with definite attempts to influence others with his opinions, but not "pushy." He is perceived by the others as warm, competent, willing to listen to others. As a result of these perceptions and evaluations, the intentions of the other members toward him are mostly friendly, with respect for his opinions, inclinations to seek his ideas and to accept his influence attempts. These intentions show in their behavior toward him, and he perceives the feedback of their behavior as telling him that he is liked and accepted, and that he is being successful in satisfying his needs to be respected and influential in the group. This feedback confirms, rather than threatens, his feelings about himself and others. So he continues to produce intentions and behaviors which are friendly, constructive, active, and influential. His position of leadership is maintained by his behavior output, by the evaluations of others, and by the flow of supportive feedback to him from the behavior of others.

Two Examples of Patterns of Low Status and Rejection in the Group

Now let's consider *Members Y and Z.*

Member Y sees himself as quite inadequate, and assumes that others see him this way also. His intentions are to be cautious, not to stick his neck out, not to try to do things or say things that will show his inadequacy or irritate others.

Member Z also feels, at a deep level, quite insecure about himself, builds a picture of himself, to himself, as quite an adequate person, but he feels that other people tend to be unfriendly and competitive (i.e., he projects his feeling of self-hatred). So his intentions, partly conscious and partly unconscious, are to keep them from blocking him, to win his way and show them how good he really is.

As you might expect, Y's behavior output is very low. He doesn't make many efforts to get into the interaction process, and is quite cautious in responding to others. He is friendly but withdrawn.

But Member Z is very active and assertive. He initiates lots of opinions, is persistent about them, and reacts critically to the ideas of others. His distrustful attitude shows up as criticalness and resistance to cooperation.

The other members don't really notice Y very much. They don't feel unfriendly, just neutral and forgetful. There really aren't many intentions for behavior toward him. Not much behavior is addressed to him.

It is different with Z. The other members feel irritated, and tend to feel rejective toward his ideas even when they are good. Their intentions are rejective and resistant. This shows up in their behavior toward him. Some ignore him and others fight him. He perceives the behavior input as a confirmation of his distrust of others, and his intentions are to be even more active in "winning his place" in spite of them. So this behavior pattern is reinforced and their evaluations are reinforced.

Y reads the relative ignoring of him by others as a confirmation of his low evaluation of himself, and feels relieved not to be the object of much attention. His behavior pattern of withdrawal is reinforced, and the group's perception of his "distance" and lack of resourcefulness is reinforced.

Summary Comments

These three brief illustrations show how the member and the group enter into a shared process of behavioral interactions and evaluations which, by partially unconscious collusion, establish a circular process that tends to reinforce and maintain the relationship between the member and the group—a relationship which is highly satisfying to some and very unsatisfying to others.

THE CIRCULAR PROCESS OF SOCIAL INTERACTION

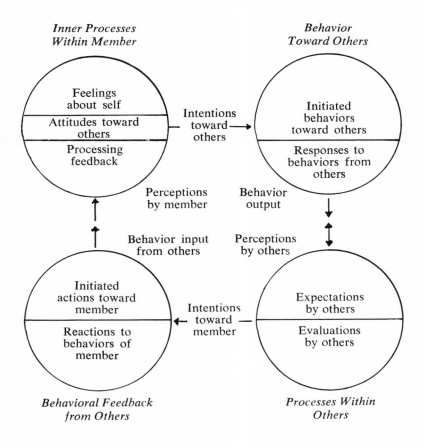

Inner Processes
Within Member

Behavior
Toward Others

Feelings
about self

Attitudes toward
others

Processing
feedback

Intentions
toward
others

Initiated
behaviors
toward others

Responses to
behaviors from
others

Perceptions
by member

Behavior
output

Behavior input
from others

Perceptions
by others

Initiated
actions toward
member

Reactions to
behaviors of
member

Intentions
toward
member

Expectations
by others

Evaluations
by others

Behavioral Feedback
from Others

Processes Within
Others

Intrapersonal and
Interpersonal Approaches

Guidelines: You may want to put the words which describe the two approaches in two columns on newsprint. *Intrapersonal* focuses on the individual, while *interpersonal* focuses on the group. Intrapersonal is developed on the basis of a medical model and counseling, while the interpersonal is developed on the basis of relational interaction and conversation. The conversational model is the one that should be used in your group. . . . I would also say that the conversational model is the hardest to do because it requires intense concentration and total involvement in the present moment. Most of us have developed a strong shell around us in order to keep us detached so that we do not take the risk of being vulnerable to others.

Intrapersonal characteristics: Focus on the there and then and deal with the question why, analysis of the problem, cause-and-effect relation, whose understanding, and whose needs. The three key words are problem, analysis, and whose understanding.

Interpersonal characteristics: Affirm the actual, which has to do with the here-and-now life and the process of this life; the meaning of the actual to each, which has to do with feedback; and a common symbol. The three key phrases are: affirm the actual, meaning to each, and common symbol

The intrapersonal, or medical, model: In this interaction a person attempts to find a problem. We tend to feel that things come alive whenever we discover a problem, particularly a personal problem. Then we feel needed. In order to locate a problem we ask the question *why* many times. Often this kind of interaction leads us to looking at the life history and the background of the person. The conversation becomes one of "there and then." The other person has the information and our job as a helper is to get the information out of the other person. The next aspect is to analyze the problem. We figure that by analyzing the problem we will eventually be able to locate the cause. Once we have discovered the cause, then we can eliminate the effect and therefore resolve the problem. This kind of interaction is based on the assumption of a scientific-medical approach. We figure we can handle the effect by locating the cause. But today science is coming to realize that many things are worked through without ever locating the cause. In fact, the question is growing whether the cause-effect approach is the best approach. It is too static and not dynamic. We are coming to see that most of life is dynamic and changing. . . .

The next aspect of this model is to get understanding. The interaction is aimed at a helper coming to understand the person with the problem. It is not that important that the person who has the problem understands. For example, when I go to a doctor I tell him what is bothering me. I tell him so he can understand me in order to give me the medicine I need. I do not need to understand what kind of medicine he is giving to me. And in this approach we constantly need to ask ourselves whose needs are being met. It is amazing how many times this model is used unconsciously to meet the needs of being wanted and being a helper of the person doing the helping rather than the person who has the problems.

I want to underline that this model is vital and very necessary.

It is definitely helpful in a counseling relationship. But we have tended to take this model and use it in all relationships. No wonder we tend to become defensive when we get even the slightest element of the personal in our conversation. We have had so many experiences in life where personal conversation and sharing led to the analytical reaction which puts both persons on the defensive.

The interpersonal, or conversational, or relational, model: First of all, this model stresses the aspect of actual life. It seeks to affirm the actual life and situation. This is very hard. When we affirm the actual, we are seeking to confirm who the other person is with all of his total existence in that moment of life. When there are a number of people present, we come to realize that each one of us has one aspect of the actual situation. The most common example is when an accident occurs and each observer of the accident has a somewhat different picture of the actual situation. In order to affirm the actual we need to focus on the here-and-now existence and the process by which we relate and have our life together more than the content. Often the actual situation is developed by indirection. We develop the skills of small talk, and through these little conversations we get impressions of each other which help us to say, this is me and this is you in our life together right now. Affirming the actual has to do with being totally aware of the other person, who is a certain size and build, wears certain clothing, and has a load of feelings.

The next element has to do with the meaning of the actual situation to each. In order for this to be accomplished we have to establish some degree of open communication so we can feed back to each other how each sees the actual situation. For example, I may be quite uncomfortable in the actual situation. The job is for me and someone else to affirm my uncomfortable feeling. Then someone and I need to look at the meaning of this feeling in the here and now. It may have to do with the fact that I am a stranger in the group and do not know the others. But the thrust of this is on what is the meaning of the actual situation and not why the person feel this way in the actual situation.

The third aspect is developing a common symbol. We will discover that by affirming the actual situation and looking at the meaning of it to each of us we will develop or create a common symbol. Each of us has given a part of ourselves to form the symbol. We discover when we meet again that this symbol becomes a bridge for communication and growth between us. Another term for the common symbol is "bond." The experience becomes a bond which holds us together. Part of the problem in life today is that there are so few common symbols which have meaning to us in the actual situation. We are spectators rather than contributors and creators of the common symbols. The expressive activities and other creative activities are opportunities where common symbols can help to identify the actual situation and provide meaning to each for his own life. Thus sometimes we start with the common symbol instead of starting with the actual affirmation of the situation. I find it very exciting to have as my job the effort of finding ways to have common symbols occur in my relationships with others. Thus conversation is not just passing the time or a bull session; instead, it becomes a search whereby each of us can become a part of the other through a common symbol. When we say, "Let's have a coke," we are using a common symbol between us. We certainly are not that interested in drinking a coke. We are actually taking the symbol as a bridge to indicate that we want to get to know each other. A handshake can be a common symbol providing it has meaning for each and has something to do with the actual experience between the two. It also can be very superficial and artificial. Part of the problem we have with the church symbols is that they have become superficial and artificial. The communion experience and the cross may be symbols of little meaning to us because we have not brought our own situation and the meaning of life into the symbol so that it becomes part of us.

A common symbol has to be specific and concrete. It has to become personal. There will occur some dynamic common symbols in your groups. Such common symbols have to do with personal experiences common to humanity. They may be death, isolation, intimacy, hate, love. I would like to encourage you to be open to common symbols and help them to develop between people.

Awareness and Sensitivity
in Interpersonal Relations

Many people get along well working with others and in all of their relationships with other people without thinking much about which foot to put forward. This seems to be what happens to us as we grow up in a society. We acquire culturally rooted ways of acting, feeling, believing, thinking, perceiving, valuing. In many ways we become encrusted with the life that goes on around us. In some respects, we may lose in this process an acute sense of our own being or identity. When difficulties arise, when the usual methods do not work—*or when we want to learn more about ourselves and others*—there is no alternative but to look at our behavior in relation to others. One of the major difficulties, however, is finding some way to think about what we know about ourselves and others, and how we can come to understand more.

One approach to problems like this is to draw a picture of it, including in our picture and our explanations of the picture the best knowledge that we have available. The diagram, known as the Johari Window, gives us a starting point.

SELF

	Known to Self	Not Known to Self
Known to Others	I Area of Free Activity	II Blind Area
Not Known to Others	III Avoided or Hidden Area	IV Area of Unknown Activity

OTHERS

We can describe the four areas in this way:

    I. The area of free activity includes behavior, thoughts, ideas, feelings, beliefs, values, motives known to me and to others.

    II. In the blind area others can see things in us of which we are unaware. We may feel one way deep down inside, but the feelings we project or describe to others may be interpreted very differently.

    III. The avoided or hidden area represents things we know but do not reveal to others. These may be our feelings or ideas. In meetings it may be some kind of hidden agenda we have that we don't want to share, or we may feel that sharing it may help defeat getting what we want.

IV. There is always an area of the unknown in human relations. Neither the individual nor others are aware of certain behavior or motives. The new, the creative, the individual, may be hidden here. We can assume their existence because these things do come to be known, and then it may be recognized that they were influencing behavior or relationships all along.

Let us briefly look at some ways in which this kind of window to reality may work.

In a New Group

In a new group, Area I is very small; there is not much free and spontaneous interaction. As the group grows and matures, Area I expands in size, and this usually means we are freer to be more like ourselves and to perceive others as they really are. Area III shrinks in size as Area I grows larger. We find it less necessary to hide or deny things we know or feel. In an atmosphere of growing mutual trust, there is less need for hiding thoughts or feelings which may be related to whatever we are concerned with. It takes longer for Area II to reduce in size, because usually there are good reasons of a psychological nature to blind ourselves to the things we feel or do. Area IV perhaps changes somewhat during our most intense learning experiences, but we can assume that such changes occur even more slowly than shifts in Area II. At any rate, Area IV is undoubtedly far larger and more influential in an individual's relationships than this sketch would indicate.

Some Principles of Change

It is obvious that for an individual or for groups of individuals, growth development, understanding, and sensitivity mean an expansion of what we here call the area of free activity. This in turn means some change in the other areas. The diagram is somewhat inadequate in that it seems to suggest what it should not—that one can draw a line around the unknown. This, of course, would be unreal. With the diagram we can point up some simple but significant principles. All of them point to the fact that we can't be human alone, and that we need other people to know ourselves.

1. A change in any one area will affect all the other areas.

2. It takes energy to hide, deny, or be blind to behavior that is involved in interaction.

3. Threat tends to decrease awareness; mutual trust tends to increase awareness.

4. Forced awareness, or forced exposure, or forced revealing of things about oneself seems to be undesirable and seems usually to be ineffective.

5. Learning means a change has taken place so that Area I is larger and one or more of the other areas has grown smaller.

6. Working with others is facilitated by a large area of free activity. This usually means that more understanding is present and more of the resources and skills of the people involved can be applied to the work at hand.

7. The smaller the area of free activity, the poorer communication is likely to be.

8. There is a universal curiosity about the unknown areas, but growth and development and understanding or sensitivity seem to be held in check by various kinds of fears, by custom, and by social training. In this case, a kind of trained capacity to see things in one way seems to develop a trained incapacity to see things in any other way.

9. Sensitivity means appreciating the concealed or covert aspects of behavior in Areas II, III, and IV, and respecting the desire of others to keep them so.

10. Learning about processes in groups as they are being

experienced helps to increase awareness (that is, to enlarge Area I) for the group as a whole as well as for individual members.

11. The value system of a group and its membership or the value system of an individual may be noted in the way unknowns in the life of the group or the individual are confronted.

12. A centipede may be perfectly happy without awareness; but after all, he restricts himself to crawling under rocks.

Expressive Behavior

Suppose that you go to a lecture delivered by a stranger. The lecture may be on any topic at all; let us say it is on "Expressive Behavior." You go primarily to hear what the lecturer will say, only secondarily, if at all, to note how he will say it. You are concerned with the content of his views. He, too, will be intent upon the subject matter.

While the lecturer is speaking, however, another process of communication is under way. Even if you are not particularly interested, you note—especially at the start of the lecture—many things about the speaker. He is tall, fairly young, neatly dressed, slender; he speaks rapidly but in a voice that is high and raspy. He repeats his phrases, smiles frequently, and mops his brow though it is not hot.

Almost immediately—whether you wish to do so or not—you get some impression about him as a person. These perceptions are fleeting, fringe-like, usually unimportant. Your judgments are shadowy and perhaps all wrong. But you cannot help making them, and he, by his expressive movements, cannot help prompting them.

Most times we are trained to pay attention to the content communication. In this study, however, we are directly interested in the style, in the expressive aspect of behavior. We are to put aside our usual preoccupation with content, with the intellectual aspects of life. We have opportunity to ask ourselves what this person's voice, speech, facial expression, style of clothing, posture, walk, and pattern of gestures signify. We sometimes think—and rightly—that the how of behavior can be more revealing than the what.

Thus expressive behavior has to do with one's style of behavior. . . . Task behavior is purposive and specifically motivated; expressive behavior is not. Task behavior is determined by the needs of the moment and by the situation; expressive behavior reflects the person. Task behavior is formally elicited; expressive behavior is spontaneously emitted. Task behavior usually aims to change the environment; expressive behavior aims at nothing, though it may incidentally have effects on the environment. Both task and expressive behavior are part of a total person. . . .

It is a tragedy of our culture that task behavior is in the ascendancy, and that creative expression is suppressed. In school young people are rigidly held to the precision of their assignment; their efforts to express their own individuality are suppressed. True, people today have more leisure, but the leisure is a matter of consuming prefabricated activities rather than having an opportunity to give individual expression. Perhaps this is why the type of dancing we see today is so expressive. An age of mechanical conformity threatens us. When expression is starved, our personalities shrivel, falling far below our human potentialities.

When I introduce expressive activities I generally indicate that this is an opportunity for us to become aware of ourselves totally as a person of God, and also how we communicate as a total person in more ways than just through words. The expressive activity can give us a chance to have an activity together in which words are not permitted, and then we have a chance to reflect verbally on the activity we experienced. Sometimes I use a statement about the brilliant thinker Einstein: "his creative thinking was not verbal but rather visual and muscular, and his words were a part of a laborious second stage of the basic insights." A ground rule for all expressive activities is that they are on a voluntary basis. A person may take part or observe as he desires. At the same time I indicate that a person will benefit most through volunteering to take part.

I am now going to describe some expressive activities. I will make no attempt to divide the expressive activity into individual activities or group activities. I will attempt to describe the activity so that a leader could give directions for persons to perform the activity. When music is used, I will try to indicate the name of the music. Loosening up exercises begin by people walking slowly around the room, greeting other people in any way a person desires. Another activity is to shake, starting with the head and eventually ending up with the foot, until a person shakes all over. Another activity is to pretend that you have a string down your back and are like a puppet. You pull yourself up with the string until you are stretching as hard as you can, and then you let the string go and collapse to the floor. Another activity is to imagine that you are holding a ball between your two hands at your waist. You let the ball bounce you to the music. Then you gradually stretch out your arms and have a ball in each hand and let the throwing of the balls back and forth from hand to hand bounce you. Another activity is to slowly imagine yourself throwing sand, throwing stones across the water, fishing with a line, throwing out a net and bringing it in. The principal background music for loosening up exercises can be *Israel Sings,* Vanguard, VRS 9118. Any type of expressive, active music is suitable.

One expressive activity used to begin building relationships is to form a circle, touching fingertips. The backs of persons are toward the center of the circle. Persons begin swaying back and forth to the music. Gradually the circle grows smaller and smaller as persons hold hands, then reach around as many others as they can. After the circle is as small as it can be, the people then gradually enlarge the circle to its original size. The second time the same process occurs, only people are facing each other and are encouraged to look into as many eyes as possible. Music for this can be *Duets with the Spanish Guitar,* Capital PA406, side 2, band 4.

Opportunity to give and receive trust can best occur in existing group. A circle is formed and a person volunteers to be moved by the pushing and guiding of other members in the circle while he keeps his eyes closed. In the second part of the activity the volunteer imagines that his feet are together in a bucket of cement. The circle becomes very tight and moves him around, back and forth, and may even lift him in the air. Members can become quite active and expressive in pushing and guiding as well as expanding the circle and letting the person go way beyond the circle. No music is needed for this activity.

Another activity helps a person become aware of his own world and the world around him. First of all, the members have their eyes closed and find some space they want to occupy—sitting on the floor or in some comfortable place. They may also want to stretch out. Then, still with eyes closed, a person explores himself and seeks to become aware of his clothing and parts of his body. When he wants to, he can then expand his world and examine the space around him and above him. He may also want to get up and seek to enter into the world of others. The duet record can be used, side 1, band 5.

A way of perceiving and soaking in the other person is to form two lines with persons facing each other. The persons directly across from each other look at each other's face and examine it as long as they desire. Then they walk toward each other as close as they want to, examine each other without touching each other, and slowly back away until they return to their original positions.

An expressive activity which helps in dealing with empathy is that of mirroring. Persons pair off, and to the rhythm of music one mirrors the other's hands and head and body as he attempts to move to the rhythm. Then this process is reversed and repeated. This activity works best when it is done two times with different persons. Background music can be duets, side 1, band 2.

One expressive activity is to utilize the world around us. This helps a person to soak in life around him and turn on his senses. One way of doing this is to give persons fifteen minutes or so to go outdoors and just walk and take in anything that attracts them. It may be something big or something very small like a leaf. The person is to take as much time as he wants to in a leisurely way, letting whatever comes to him stick with him for a while.

An activity which helps to illustrate the value of aggression in relationships, and that conflict can be constructive is the following. Persons pair off, mainly according to height. Then one person takes the initiative and attempts to push the other person to the floor until the person is flat on the floor. The person being pushed can resist in any way he desires. The person doing the pushing can attempt to get the person to the floor in any way he desires as long as no physical harm occurs. Then the person who did the pushing has to get the other person back to an upright position. Then the activity is reversed within the pair.

The following expressive activity occurs best in a group that has been together for a while. A person volunteers and closes his eyes. The rest of the group lifts him in the air, stretching him out parallel to the floor. To the music the group gently rocks him back and forth and, as slowly as possible, lowers him to the floor. This exercise is very supportive, very warm, both emotionally and physically, and is an opportunity to receive and give acceptance, affection, and trust. The background music suggested is *Miriam Makeba,* RCA LPM 2267, side 1, band 2, Suliram.

An expressive activity which helps us to utilize our imaginations is a fantasy. Persons find a position in which they feel comfortable. They close their eyes and simply listen to music and let the music lead them wherever it will. Afterward they are to share with two or three other persons what they visualized in the fantasy. You may want to ask them if they saw people, colors, or settings. The background music for this can be Holst's *The Planets,* Capitol PA 385, side 1, band 2.

Above all, it must be kept in mind that these expressive activities are not to be forced. They have opportunity for us to enjoy something and see what will happen. If nothing happens, that is quite satisfactory. The expressive activities give us an occasion to have fun and play. We are realizing today that much individuality and creative insight occurs through the spirit of play. Also, it must be kept in mind that the expressive activities are not aimed at analyzing a person. We are so obsessed in our society with analysis that we become defensive. The thrust is simply to share ourselves and the feelings we have. This in itself is hard for us to do but very valuable in helping us to gain self-confidence and to become more expressive.

Negativity

One of the most powerful forces in group life is the factor of negativity—one person differing with another. It is at once perhaps both the most potentially destructive force in human relations and the most potentially creative.

Whether negativity and opposition shall be destructive or creative depends essentially on the nature of our response to it. And the nature of our response will be determined in large part by the value judgment we place on negativity.

If we think people who oppose us are utterly wrong, we will erect a counter opposition and resist them. This is to place a low value on negativity.

If we succumb to opposition, we die.

If we will assume that some measure of truth is probably to be found in all negativity, we will be receptive to enabling this truth to be released and thus put the negativity to creative use.

You have never really understood or accepted opposition until you have so savored the flavor of this position that you begin to feel the pull of its persuasion.

Thus there are essentially three responses we can make to negativity:

1. Resist it.
2. Succumb to it.
3. Deal with it creatively.

Every effort of man to state the truth is limited; the ability to act in accord with this limited apprehension of truth is likewise limited; consequently, opposition encountered in group life is both inevitable and desirable; hence, opposition should be neither resisted nor succumbed to, but dealt with creatively.

This for us can only come in relation to the Christian doctrines of God and man. This is twofold:

1. Our finiteness. We are not God; not in possession of absolute truth; not able to discern truth absolutely. God alone is All (all-knowing, all-powerful, always present). God's revelation of himself has been granted us, but we have not fully comprehended, nor desired, nor accepted the revelation.

2. The fact and barrier of our sin. Our motives are never all-pure. Always being victims of ourselves to some degree and always the victims of selfishness, we are incapable of making observations which will be absolute in their hold on the truth.

The course of negativity:

1. The expression of an idea always calls forth an opposing idea or series of ideas which strike some kind of balance (not necessarily equality) or adjustment to each other.

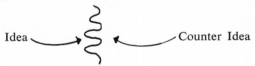

2. Ideas are always expressed by *persons,* and to some degree when one person's idea is opposing another person's idea, the person is also opposing the other person.

3. Task needs and individual needs blend or become confused in the propagation of any idea, and either may be in the ascendant. Perception is blurred and hostility is usually present as ideas which appear to have an *intellectual source* have a personal or feeling source, and ideas which ostensibly are directed at other ideas are in reality being directed at a person.

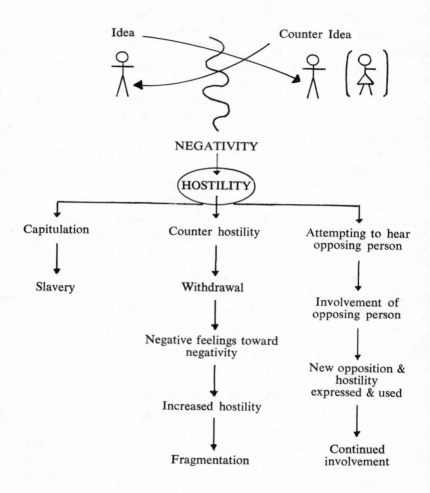

The Ministry
of Helping

Objectives: To describe some factors involved in a helping relationship.

To present the concept of force field as an aid to analysis of change.

To look at some of the religious aspects of the change relationship.

To become a Christian is to be changed. Being changed persons, we find we are led to help other persons change and grow as persons in Christ. Leadership and teaching in the simplest definition are helping persons make desirable changes. So God calls us to enter into a ministry of helping—providing relationships with others whereby a person or group is helped to change.

As in every relationship which involves change—whether with persons or groups—the change may be both wished and feared. The problem for which help is desired is brought to the helper, but at the same time inner resources of the person or group are usually developed which are to defend the existing situation. In effect, the person or group that receives the ministry of helping seems to want the new without any essential giving up of the old—to change and yet not to change.

I. Some Assumptions

A. Change is a necessary part of life if we are going to live and grow as Christians.

    B. No person or group is exempt from the results of change. Thus what affect one part affects the whole situation.

    C. The behavior of individuals and groups can be changed.

    D. The effects of change can be predicted somewhat—perhaps more than is first assumed.

II. A Description of the Helping Relationship in a Change Situation

Learning is self-directed change in behavior. Actually neither you nor I can make changes in anyone. In Christian growth, only God can change persons. Too often in the change we have oversimplified the matter by thinking all we have to do is to pipe out the information and, presto, people will change! But the evidence shows that the desired changes have not taken place. Our task is the delicate and sensitive one of providing helping relationships whereby people open their lives to the guidance of the Holy Spirit. We can't do this through coercion or force; each person must make his own response. But what we can do is to provide a helping relationship whereby the person or group has the opportunity to change.

    A. Before a person initiates a helping relationship for change, he must examine—

        1. *His assumptions about persons.* The attitude of a leader toward other persons is probably more critical than the nature of the change itself. If a helper sees his job only as an opporunity to reinforce certain types of words or opinions in others, then he tends to confirm the person receiving help only as an object—a basically mechanical, manipulatable object. If this is the potentiality the helper sees in the other, the other tends to act in a manner which supports the assumption of the helper. However, if the helper sees the relationship as an opportunity to reinforce

all that the other is, with all his existent potentialities, then he tends to act in ways which support this assumption. In the second assumption the helper confirms the other as a living person, capable of creative inner development.

2. *The value of the goal* the helper is seeking in the relationship. Whose needs are being met? The leader needs to be aware of his own needs and make sure his needs are not the only concern for the change desired.

3. *The importance of the change itself.* Of what significance is the change desired?

B. Begin the helping effort at the point where the helping agent is in that situation where he can make reliable predictions about the consequences of his actions. For most of us this point of contact is within the day-by-day relationships with others.

C. Seek to establish a relationship of acceptance with persons or groups. The more acceptance I feel toward others, the more I will be creating a relationship of acceptance. By acceptance I mean a warm regard for him as a person of unconditional self-worth—of value no matter what his condition, his behavior, or his feelings. It means a respect and liking for the other as a separate person, a willingness for him to possess his own feelings in his own way. It includes an acceptance of and a regard for his attitudes of the moment, no matter how negative or positive, no matter how much they may contradict other attitudes he has held in the past. This acceptance of each fluctuating aspect of this other person provides for him a relationship of warmth and safety; the safety of being liked and prized as a person seems a highly important factor in a helping relationship.

"With loving respect for personality, Jesus appreciated all persons as they were at the moment. Having a deep-rooted belief in the possibilities of human beings, he could look beyond their present state of achievement to what they were capable of becoming." (*Learning to Lead*, p. 71.)

If we recognize that our commitment to a ministry of helping puts us in a position of potential change agents, then the question usually asked is: "What right have I to try to make people different than they are?" This must be reversed. The basic question which cannot be avoided is: "In a changing situation, what right have I to withhold myself, my skills and my convictions, from helping that change to take place in a direction consistent with my convictions (faith)?"

The major consideration, therefore, is whether or not one acts consistent with his faith. The helper has a demand on him to be a *faith-full* person in his response to the situation needing change. Refusal to act because of the risk involved—and faith *does* involve risk—is to act *un*faithfully. God asks of each of us that we make a faithful response to the life given to him.

Being a helper costs in terms of time and effort. It also costs in terms of emotional energy through the acceptance of the feelings of others. These may be either hostile or overly dependent and affectionate. In a very real sense the helper must be willing to suffer. Because we tend to sin against relationships, both the other person and the helper will tend to sin against each other. One may attempt to exploit the other or treat with irreverence this child of God. Such suffering seems inevitable on the part of both participants. A measuring of the ability of each to withstand the cost is needed before commitment to the planning of change takes place. It may be only through the acceptance of the act of redemption, available to each of us, that the helper and those to be helped can enter into such a relationship under the knowledge that suffering can take place.

Finally, the change agent involved in a ministry to help is able to enter into the relationship of change because he believes in the potentiality residing within the relationship for the operation of the Holy Spirit. The change agent can enter into and leave the process of change without excessive anxiety because he trusts both the working of the Holy Spirit and the inner-workings of the other persons. Change is entered into with the confidence of those involved, because they inhabit a co-personal world where each may enable the others involved to achieve in some degree his God-given potential. The helper enters this ministry recognizing that the Holy Spirit works through others as well as himself, and he is prepared for this experience. The helper and others can become instruments in an enabling relationship which can embody the Holy Spirit in such a way that all may respond increasingly as whole persons and enter into creative dialogue with one another and with God. Each may be re-created by the Spirit and achieve in some measure his God-given potentiality.

Loneliness
and the Capacity to Love

I shall give an example from psychotherapy of possession by a state not commonly considered daimonic—namely, loneliness. In this patient, attacks of acute loneliness, developing into panic, were not infrequent. He could not orient himself in the panics, could not hang on to his sense of time, and became, as long as the bout of loneliness lasted, numb in his reactions to the world. . . . He tried desperately to fight off these attacks—as we all do, which is not surprising since acute loneliness seems to be the most painful kind of anxiety which a human being can suffer. . . .

This patient would try, when the loneliness began, to wrench his mind away to thoughts about something else, to get busy doing work or go out to a movie—but no matter what escape he tried, there remained the haunting, satanic menace hovering behind him like a hated presence waiting to plunge a rapier into his lungs. . . .

But one day, he came in reporting that he had made a surprising discovery. When an acute attack of loneliness was beginning, it occurred to him not to try to fight it off—running had never helped anyway. Why not accept it, breathe with it, turn toward it and not away? Amazingly, the loneliness did not over-

From *Love and Will* by Rollo May, pp. 150–153. By permission of W. W. Norton & Co., 55 Fifth Avenue, New York, N.Y. 10003.

whelm him when he confronted it directly. Then it seemed even to diminish. Emboldened, he began to invite it by imagining situations in the past when he was acutely lonely, the memories of which had, up to now, always been sure to cue off the panic. But strangely enough, the loneliness had lost its power. He couldn't feel the panic even when he tried. The more he turned on it and welcomed it, the more impossible it was even to imagine how he'd ever been lonely in that unbearably painful way before.

The patient had discovered—and was teaching me that day— that he felt the acute loneliness only as he ran; when he turned on the "devil," it vanished. . . . The very running is a response which assures the daimonic of its obsessive power. . . . The anxiety (or loneliness) has the upper hand as long as we continue to run.

Anxiety (loneliness or "abandonment anxiety" being its most painful form) overcomes the person to the extent that he loses orientation in the objective world. To lose the world is to lose one's self, and vice versa; self and world are correlates. The function of anxiety is to destroy the self-world relationship, i.e., to disorient the victim in space and time and, so long as this disorientation lasts, the person remains in the state of anxiety. . . . Now if the person can reorient himself . . . and again relate himself to the world directly, experientially, with his senses alive, he overcomes the anxiety. . . . [He can take] practical steps when he experiences anxiety such as stopping and asking just what it was that occurred in reality or in his fantasies that preceded the disorientation which cued off the anxiety. He is not only opening the doors of his closet where the ghosts hide, but he often can also take steps to reorient himself in his practical life . . .

Still looking at my patient who had been obsessed with loneliness, let us ask, What was the constructive side of this daimonic which presumably had gone awry? Being a sensitive, gifted person, he had achieved notable success in practically all realms of human experience except personal intimacy. His gifts included a capacity for interpersonal empathy and a good deal of tenderness—most of which had been absorbed in his self-preoccupation. He had failed to use his capacities for relationship; he had been unable to open himself up to others, to reach out to them, to share feelings and other aspects of personal experience, to identify with and affirm them in the ways necessary to build durable relationship. In short, what he had lacked, and now needed, was the exercise of his capacities to love in an active, outgoing concern for the other's welfare, for the sharing of pleasure and delight as an "I" with "Thou," for a communion of consciousness with his fellows. The daimon, in the constructive sense in this case and put in the simplest terms, was his potentiality for active loving.

Questions: Have you ever experienced loneliness of this sort? If so, how did you deal with it? Have you ever fled from loneliness by increased activity of any kind? What? How successful was this attempt? How did you feel about it? Explain in your own words how this man dealt with his loneliness? What allowed him to do so? Is his "answer" in any way helpful to you? Why?

Dialogue with Fear

SK: I wish I could begin by saying, "Damn you, fear. Leave me alone!" but honesty demands that I address you as "Dear fear," for you have been with me most of my life. Now I want to understand why I am attracted to you and did not banish you long ago.

FEAR: I am glad you are willing to admit that we are reluctant friends. It has taken me some years to get you to confess that you are a hesitant lover of what you pretend to despise. What a capacity for self-deceit you have, pretending that I was somehow your fated enemy! Or, to be specific, that I was an unconscious legacy from your parents. Such transparent nonsense. If I am your fate, I am at least a fate you have chosen and nurtured. It is not without your consent and satisfaction that we have been together all these years. You might have lived in conversation with love, or courage, or creativity, or desire, or fame. No! You have kept me around. So don't try to disown me.

SK: O.K. you have me. I admit some responsibility for continually talking with you but I certainly do not get satisfaction from your presence. You are like a bad neighbor. I am stuck with you but I wish you would move away.

"Dialogue with Fear" (pp. 109–112), from *To a Dancing God* by Sam Keen. Copyright © 1970 by Sam Keen. By permission of Harper & Row, Publishers, Inc., 10 East 53rd Street, New York, N.Y. 10022.

FEAR: You lie easily. The fact is I am a valuable companion and a loyal friend. I don't demand change of you. I am satisfied to keep your relation as it has always been. I do not ask you to venture out into the unknown or act heroically in defining your existence in the carelessness and caprice of the world. All I ask is a token, a ritual, a guarantee that you will not go beyond the limits I have set for your comfort and safety.

SK: Ritual or token, hell! You demand the most alive part of me. Your "token" is the whole of my capacity for new experience. You promise security so long as I surrender my autonomy, my critical ability, my reason, my responsibility for reflecting upon and evaluating my own experience. Your price for comfort is giving up growth.

FEAR: So what if the price is high? If you refuse to acknowledge my authority you will fall into pride and rebellion. I keep the boundaries. I set the limits. Only Adam, Prometheus, and other proud but foolish rebels have the illusion that they are strong enough to define the nature of good and evil for themselves. No man, and least of all you, has the wisdom, the energy, or the time to determine the limits of the possible for himself. Such omnipotent pretense is clearly sinful and stupid.

SK: You sound so reasonable and charitable. But, in truth, you wear the face of the Grand Inquisitor. You would refuse me knowledge of my freedom in exchange for comfort, and thus steal my dignity and potency.

FEAR: Can you deny that both humility and wisdom are on the side of the Inquisitor? Yes, I speak with the voice of authority. I echo the commands and prohibitions of your parents. But I speak as *your* past, *your* tradition. If I limit you to the possibilities which were conceivable to your parents, it is merely to enforce those rules and limits they found necessary to the fullness of life. My voice is conservative. I would have you love what your fathers loved and hate what they hated, for there is wisdom in the experience of the generations which is absent in the individual. I preserve your energies from being dissipated in folly.

sk: The limits of the possible change. Human nature is not static. What was psychologically inconceivable to my parents is an open possibility for me, except when you intervene.

fear: I am glad you spoke about "the limits of the possible." You are aware that Camus used this phrase as a summary of his philosophy of life. Now—can you tell me in all honesty that you are willing to face the uncertainty, the tentativeness, the absolute demand for self-definition in the face of the absurd that was his daily bread and wine? If not, don't pretend that you want me to leave you altogether, because I protect you against this horrible vacuum of the unknown. I give you ground upon which to stand in the swirl. Even if it is sometimes bitter ground, it is a place for your feet. Better fear than anxiety, better a hostile force at the center of your personality than the emptiness which is the promise of death, better pain than chaos. The suffering I cause is only a necessary by-product of enforcing the limits which give you definition and succor.

sk: I do not accept your way. Granted, I must have limits or else I would explode into the void of infinite possibility and schizophrenia. However, there is a better way to establish boundaries than you suggest. *Decision* is the alternative to fear. I can take upon myself the responsibility for deciding, and then the pain of limitation is not imposed but chosen. Maturity rather than fate or fear may determine the shape my life will assume. Your presence is not necessary.

fear: I will admit this heroic possibility exists. Should you choose to accept full responsibility for your values and decisions, I will leave you. But I will always be waiting for your energies to give out. Few persons manage the heroic style of total responsibility. I doubt that you can abide by this high ideal. At any rate, we are talking in theoretical terms. As of this moment, you are still engaged in dialogue with me. If the time comes when you choose to be fascinated by love, or creativity, or even work, I will leave you alone. For the time being we remain reluctant friends.

SK: I accept your conclusion with sadness. Nevertheless, I must say, you begin to bore me. Perhaps tomorrow I will converse with you less, and the day after not at all.

FEAR: We shall see.

Approach II

BIBLE STUDY

This section may be of help if you plan to build your group sessions primarily around Bible study. Here you will find specific suggestions for nine sessions related to the three major areas of study in the student's text (pp. 43–139). The students should be encouraged to read the first two sections, however, and this would be an appropriate assignment prior to the first session, if books are distributed ahead of time.

While your detailed Bible study will begin with chapter 3 of the text, it would be wise to take time in the first class meeting after chapters 1 and 2 have been read to deal with questions the students have on these two chapters, whether they are questions simply for clarification or are about the content, the ideas set forth. This is important for two reasons: (1) the material in the first two sections helps prepare the way for the rest of the book, and study of the last three sections will be more meaningful if the earlier material is understood; and (2) if people have unanswered questions that they are really concerned about, they may find it difficult to move ahead wholeheartedly until these questions are dealt with or at least acknowledged. But you will want to help students see that your primary focus is on the Biblical materials in chapters 3–8, and that study of these chapters will throw light on the first two; therefore, since many of their concerns will be dealt with in the sessions that follow, they do not have to have exhaustive analysis at the first session. With this assurance, the class may be content to have their questions recorded, with the promise that if they do not come up naturally, they will be dealt with before the sessions end. Thus you may be able to limit discussion of chapters 1–2 to questions of clarification and move on to the Bible study.

GENERAL PROCEDURE

The general procedure for this series of Bible studies might be as follows:

1) Where the Bible assignment is lengthy, as in session A below, assign the Biblical material for *advance* study. Be as specific as possible in the assignment—what precisely should the students be looking and listening for as they study?

2) Where the passages are brief, as in session B, you can dispense with advance study (that would be a good time for students to read the appropriate chapter in the text), and engage in study and discussion within the class session. If you choose this route, the following steps provide one means for fruitful study.

a) If class members do not have a strong foundation for Bible study, you may need to place the passages within the context of the total Christian message before actual study begins.

b) Ask each person to read silently the passages to be studied.

c) Then ask them to paraphrase the passage in modern terms and to find the central point of the passage. In this process they should identify any difficult words needing further clarification, or traditional words of the faith which are often used with little understanding. Participants should be instructed to translate, in paraphrasing, traditional words into new ones which say what is meant in a new way.

d) Ask participants to identify the following (have questions posted for all to see):

What do I not understand about the passage?

What of particular importance is being said?

What does this passage say to me personally? What does it imply for my life?

e) Ask individuals to share their findings, and according to what has been discovered, use questions suggested in the session plans to help your group explore further implications of the passages.

Optional Activities

NOTE: a group can with profit focus its study on the Biblical material given at the close of each chapter, but members' experience will be greatly enriched if they also read the chapters themselves and participate in some of the exercises described earlier in this text.

1) Encourage the students to read the chapter in the text during the period that your Bible study is based on that chapter. Time must then be allowed for questions for clarification and for discussion of the general content of the chapter in light of the Biblical studies that are the primary focus of your sessions.

2) In each session plan, one or more experience-centered exercises from the first part of this leader's guide are noted to indicate possible learning experiences of a different type that might well be used in conjunction with the Bible study. Of course, you and your class can best decide when the use of one or more of these exercises would be of benefit.

SPECIFIC SESSION PLANS

Sessions related to "Loneliness—Love—Communication":

SESSION A

Focus: Jesus Christ as love in action.

(Experience session 2, exercises 2 and 4; session 3, exercises 1 and 2)

This session deals with the participants' study of the life of Jesus. Assign one of the Gospels, with the questions given in "For Further Study," No. 1, on page 54 of the participant's book. Discuss the Gospel in class in light of those questions and the ones found under No. 1 on page 78.

SESSION B

Focus: The function of understanding and forgiveness in love of others.

(Experience session 2, exercises 1, 2, 4; session 3, exercises 1 and 2; session 4, exercise 2)

This study centers on passages listed in No. 2 of "For Further Study," page 54. The following questions could direct movement of discussion after Bible study: What role does empathetic understanding, which seeks to enter into the other person's feelings, play in love? How is it possible to judge actions as right or wrong (moral or immoral) while at the same time understanding and not judging the person? What role does forgiveness play in love relationships? Explain why it is a necessary element in human love relationships. Does forgiveness in love really call forth love from the person receiving it, or does it simply say to that person that anything goes?

SESSION C

Focus: The function of understanding and forgiveness in love of one's self.

(Experience session 4, exercise 1)

This session deals with passages suggested in No. 2 of "Awareness Triggers," page 73. The following questions may be helpful in directing discussion after study of the passages: Is it really necessary to recognize specifics of "the sin" that lies within each of us before we can truly love ourselves or others? Explain your answer. What makes it so hard to receive forgiveness from others? from one's own self? In what ways does real, experiential reception of God's forgiving love free one for growth in love?

Sessions related to "Anxiety—Courage—Actualization":

SESSION D

Focus: Finding security and courage in God.
(Experience session 6, exercises 1 and 2)

One or two study sessions could center on the passages listed in "For Further Study," page 89. In each of the Psalms listed, the psalmist indicates some aspect of his experience of God that has provided courage and security for his personal life. Have class participants list these sources of courage and security. Then discuss *how* these experiences of God strengthen the person for life. Do they remove all uncertainties in life? If not, what do they do?

Next, study the New Testament passages. Then indicate that obviously faith in God does not remove all anxiety from finite life. You might give some examples to illustrate the point. Then ask: How does a personal experience of the God revealed in Christ give people strength for confident life? What kind of secure faith in God is suggested by each passage? How does that security free us to live within the anxiety of life?

SESSION E

Focus: Security in one's God-given self.
(Experience session 6, exercises 1, 2, 3, 4; session 7, exercise 4)

One session might be developed around Scripture suggested in No. 1 of "For Further Study," page 105. Let discussion flow around these two central questions: Explain how knowledge of our true nature and destiny revealed in Scripture frees us to confront the anxieties of fate, emptiness, and guilt. In what ways does the frank recognition of our sins and our acceptance of God's love free us from the paralyzing effects of anxiety? In order to keep this discussion from disintegrating into mere intellectual play, you may need from time to time to interject, "But pratically, in real life, how does that really help?" Then call to mind any problem area that will clarify the issue. For example: "But suppose I've accepted a very difficult task, and all of a sudden, I'm not doing well in it. Gradually I find myself being immobilized, unable to take any kind of action. My perception gets distorted and I begin to fear not only that I will not be able to accomplish this task, but that, indeed, I'm becoming a *nothing* who can *do* nothing. How can knowledge of my true nature and destiny help me out of that situation?" Of course, your examples will need to be geared to the discussion, but you could think of some possible examples before class session.

A second session on this same focus could flow from study of passages suggested in No. 3 of "For Further Study," page 106. Ask participants to compare the truths Jesus is pointing out with the affirmations of psychologists, who say that anxiety can be met constructively if a person is developing and using his potentialities, but that if a person fails to develop his capacities, he becomes sick and unable to cope with the anxieties of life. After this comparison, ask persons to share any real-life illustrations of these truths which come to mind. Then indicate that these teachings of Jesus, studied by themselves, contain a real element of threat: "If you don't produce, you'll become a nothing. You'll be cut down." What other teachings of Jesus allow people to deal with that threat and the anxiety it produces? In other words, what other teachings become sources of courage which can free people to risk-taking responsibility for developing their full potential? How do they encourage us?

The session might be closed by asking each person to think of one area of undeveloped potential he would like to begin to develop. If there is time, each person might like to share his hope with the class.

SESSION F
FOCUS: Freedom in Christ.
(Experience session 6, exercises 1, 3, 4)

A study about the paradoxical nature of freedom in Christ could flow from study of the Scriptures suggested in No. 2 of "For Further Study," page 106. These are difficult passages focusing on a complex concept and reality; consequently, it would probably be good to assign advance study of the passages. In addition, you might ask one or two persons to really dig into background study through commentaries.

After coming to an understanding of the passages, relate those truths to psychological insights talked about in "Acting in Finite Freedom," pages 94–95, by using the questions in No. 2 of "For Further Study."

Sessions related to "Emptiness—Integration—Valuing":

All sessions in this section would probably be most effective after some exercises from experience sessions 8, 9, and 10.

SESSION G
FOCUS: How did Jesus view man's ethical responsibility?

A discussion session could be developed around the comparative study suggested in No. 1 of "For Further Study," page 118. If you decide this study would be helpful for your group, you will need to assign in advance the reading of a Gospel in the light of the eight statements about Jesus' teachings. (The latter should be duplicated and distributed.) If people select different Gospels, this should enrich the discussion. In the class session, divide the group into smaller units for work. One group could evaluate statements a–d, another e–g, and a third group could tackle the summary statement, h. Ask groups (1) to decide whether they think the statements are valid reflections on the life and teachings of Jesus, and (2) to say why the statements seem to them correct or incorrect.

Allow fifteen to twenty minutes for small group discussion; then ask each group to share its findings. Allow time for people to react to the findings of other groups. Then move on to see if the class can come to agreement by formulating a group answer to the question, How did Jesus view man's ethical responsibility?

If time permits, the sessions could be concluded by (1) asking each person who will to contribute at least one implication of the answer just formulated for his own life, or (2) having the class evaluate its answer against May's two questions quoted on page 120.

SESSION H

FOCUS: How does Christ free men for mature valuing?

This session would center on an in-class depth study of the Scripture suggested in No. 1 of "For Further Study," page 136. (If you do not think time will permit study of all passages, omit Matthew 26:26–28 and Hebrews 10:11–31.) After study of the passages, conclude by discussing the questions in 2 and 3 of "For Further Study." Throughout this discussion, strive to move from the theoretical realm to the practical by interjecting or asking for concrete, everyday examples of "freedom from sin for new life," "the conscience transformed by Christ," etc.

SESSION I

FOCUS: Maturing sons, responsible to God.

This session could begin with an in-depth study of Genesis 1:28, Galatians 3:23—4:7, and Romans 8:18–25. See No. 4 of "For Further Study," page 137.

Next, ask the class to formulate a statement which indicates as clearly and specifically as possible how a Christian in today's world can use his freedom as a responsible child and heir of God. Ask participants to keep this statement before them as you move on to the next part of the activity.

Distribute copies of recent newspapers to class members. Divide the class into two units. Ask one group to follow instructions given in No. 1a of "Action Learning," page 135, and the other to follow instructions in No. 1b. (If your time is limited, you may need to select several articles prior to class session and bring them rather than entire newspapers.) After groups have had time to make decisions about how a child of God might respond to these current situations, ask each group to report its findings.

Approach III

DISCUSSION OF THE TEXT

Listed below are a number of films which could be used to stimulate thought and discussion centered on specific concerns dealt with in the participant's book. The films do not give answers but could be used as openers. From discussion of these films, participants could move into discussion of the content of the text. (NOTE: In all discussion sessions, participants should have their books at hand so that they can refer to quotations, diagrams, etc.)

You, of course, will need to preview the films and work out a series of questions about the films and other questions which relate to the text. This work before class is essential. A simple "Well, what was the film saying?" or "What do you think?" rarely produces depth responses. Think through: Where does the film hit us in our struggle to become human? What very human concerns, problems, feelings, does it deal with? Then create questions which will help persons explore these areas. Always try to move discussion from the theoretical to the practical, everyday, feeling-action level.

In addition to film listings for each major area of book content, you will find a series of questions related to the book. These questions focus on concerns which may need further discussion in class. They may or may not be the ones your class needs to think through. Only you can be the final judge. (Needless to say, the questions can be used without using a film.)

INTRODUCTORY SESSIONS RELATED TO SECTIONS 1 AND 2

"Homo Homini" (11 min., color; can be rented together with "Acceleration"). This film would be a provocative tool for a beginning session before your actual study begins. It is a strange, highly dramatic allegorical tale of man and his technology. It points up many of the dehumanizing factors of contemporary society and raises the question of what it means to be human. An excellent discussion film.

"Acceleration" (3 min., color, animation). This is a witty cartoon that makes a very serious point—that man, for all his progress, has still not fathomed the mystery of himself.

"This Solitude Through Which We Go Is I!" (30 min., B&W). This film could also be used with chapters 3 and 4. The emphasis of the film is on the kinds of things that happen in the world every day. On anonymous locations, anonymous participants share the drama of earthly ecstasy and suffering. This candid, quick approach stirs up a real sense of solitude. We are brought very close to people we will never know; then when we are quickly snatched away from them, most sensitive persons can't resist the feeling of longing amid the solitude of which the title speaks.

"The Stringbean" (17 min., B&W and color). In this lovely bit of visual poetry we are made to understand that as a stringbean stalk grows out of just a tiny seed, so human beings can persistently penetrate the cells of solitude into which circumstances have forced them. The film bends your ears and eyes with gentle persuasion toward the discerning line between real living and mere existence. Black and white and color are used to delineate respectively the contrasts between the private world of hope and longing and the outside world of encounter with nature and persons.

Questions for "So God Created Man"

1) Which, if any, of the brief descriptions of modern man in "Prophets of Our Time" seem particularly true of life as you experience it? Give examples to illustrate your answer.
2) Do you think there are aspects of twentieth-century life which make it particularly difficult for individuals to live meaningful, fruitful lives? If so, what are they?
3) In what ways do you think the insights gained by psychology might be of help to persons seeking to become responsible children of God?
4) Your class could explore and analyze together the diagram on page 23; then ask what various levels of truth it calls to people's minds from their own experience.

Questions for "One Self or Many?"

1) What basic aspects of human existence make the process of becoming human difficult?
2) Explain why you agree or disagree with this statement: Self-deception is inevitable in human life since true self-knowledge includes acceptance of an ambiguous, threatening human condition which man always seeks to avoid.
3) In what sense is "becoming an integrated whole" a major task for the human being?
4) Do you agree that it is difficult for a person to accept and choose to be the self he truly is? Why?
5) Explain how a warm, accepting, understanding relationship can free a person "to become more and more himself." Can you think of any life illustrations of Rogers' statement, "We can-

not move away from what we are, until we thoroughly *accept* what we are"? What does this statement have to do with God's forgiving love?

6) In what sense is self-knowledge "a response to divine revelation"?

"LONELINESS—LOVE—COMMUNICATION"

"Everyday Chronicle" (11 min., color, animation). A very sad, touching little story, in animation that is deliberately topsy-turvy and handled with the utmost skill. The modern city is looked upon as a gigantic turnstile through which people pass who are so myopic that the identity of all creatures, both man and beast, is lost. Yet the film warms us with the feeling that the love of one being for another can persist.

"A Chairy Tale" (10 min., B&W). In this imaginative film a young man and an ordinary straight chair have an encounter. There are many levels at which the film can be read—as pure farce, as a kind of ballet, as an exercise in perception, as a symbolic suggestion of various kinds of relationships. Hopefully it will be a moving experience for anyone who sees it, alerting him personally to some new moral, ethical, social, or religious imperatives. It speaks a kind of mysterious language out of somebody's sense of total, if sometimes reluctant, involvement with the world, and the reality of Buber's 1-Thou encounter that he has found there.

Questions

1) In what ways do you see love as a problem in today's world?
2) How do most contemporary people seem to try to overcome their separation from others?
3) Is love the only activity which can overcome one's separateness in a fulfilling manner? Explain your thinking.
4) Why do you agree or disagree with Fromm's statement, "Love is primarily giving, not receiving"?

5) Do you think it is necessary for one to love himself if he is to love others? Why?

6) In actual experience, how does God's love free men to love?

7) Is love possible without honest, open, mutual revelations of persons? Explain your answer by giving life examples.

8) Is true self-knowledge really the beginning of growth and change? Why or why not?

9) Does true self-knowledge come only through open communication with others? Explain.

10) Evaluate the statements about intimacy-level communication (p. 60). Is this too idealistic? Can people actually communicate at this level without alienating others?

11) Think about God's open disclosure of himself in Jesus Christ. What relationship do you see between this self-revelation and the thoughts about depth communication?

"ANXIETY—COURAGE—ACTUALIZATION"

"In the Kitchen" (12 min., B&W, no dialogue). This film shows in juxtaposition two different life-styles—life that is neat, ordered, with roles well assigned, sometimes monotonous, alongside life that is passionate, adventurous, chancy, sometimes very heartbreaking. They are the yin and yang of human existence from which everyone must choose or form a personal synthesis.

"Run!" (16 min., B&W). This film (which could also be used with the next section) is an excellent example of Theater of the Absurd. Disjointed episodes, at first confusing and laughable, are woven into a quiltwork of horror, culminating in the destruction of a human being. Life, the film seems to say, can be a relentless race through hostile streets and freaky sideshows. With no time to step back and observe the strings that manipulate us, the disintegration of our souls can be prorated over a lifetime. The film is an overstatement, but in allegorical form many facets of the confusion of modern life are viewed.

"Between the Cup and the Lip" (11 min., color, animation). A very unusual but effective type of translucent animation is used in this very somber, dirge-like film on death. Death is considered the intruder in life, the curse that keeps man from soaring like a bird, and it is compared to the master cardplayer who holds the one and only ace of spades.

"Very Nice, Very Nice" (8 min., B&W). The sporadic fears, doubts, and anxieties that are commonly suffered by twentieth-century people are given tongue-in-cheek attention in a brilliant collage, with varied visual techniques used for emphasis. One can sense the conflicting movements of people seeking pleasure and the good life, while on another level of consciousness they know that there is a price tag on all their dreams and desires. (This film could also be used with chapters 7 and 8.)

Questions

1) What is anxiety? Why is it a normal part of human life?
2) What are the effects of anxiety upon the human being? Give some real-life examples.
3) Why is it so difficult for one "to choose to be himself"?
4) Why is it so hard for a person to accept the limitations of finite freedom? Are the limitations really that confining?
5) How can one overcome the devastating effects of anxiety? Give real-life examples.
6) How does God extend to us the courage and power to become in spite of the insecurities of finite life? How is this experienced in life?

"EMPTINESS—INTEGRATION—VALUING"

"Note from Above" (2 min., color, animation). A somewhat controversial film which would certainly stimulate discussion related to how man knows truth—how he decides what is right or wrong. It strikes out at religious legalism and literalism, pointing out that truth to be "revealed" must be affirmed in human experience.

"Decoration" (7 min., color, animation). Is virtue its own reward? Or is it as destructive as any other form of obsession if it in fact becomes an obsession? The basic question of morality is penetrated, and the compulsive forms of it are separated from its creative forms. The film ought to prove provocative, as well as unnerving, to all sensitive, thinking people.

"The Good Life" (22 min., B&W). This discussion film looks at the alienation of the individual in a mass society. An average middle-class family man plays hooky from his job one day in order to search for meaning to his life as it is motivated by the values of the society of which he is a part. In the end, he returns to work and resumes his everyday routine, having found no solution to the dilemma.

Questions

1) What personal examples of emptiness and loss of meaning do you see in today's world? How do you think most people have acquired the values they do hold? Do these values seem to be the integrating core of their lives?
2) Do you think values, goals, and meanings are really very important for human growth and development? Why?
3) Explain why you agree or disagree with Rogers when he says that the usual adult has abdicated his role as a responsible valuer.
4) Does Rogers' description of the valuing process in the mature adult seem selfish? Why?
5) What do you think of Rogers' statement that in the mature person values are not held rigidly but are continually changing? Is this "good" or "bad"?
6) Do you agree that man can enter into dialogue with God and actually decide for himself what love demands in a particular

situation? If so, what is the purpose of the commandments and teachings of Jesus?

7) What kind of growth climate do you think should be created to enable persons to develop as responsible sons of God?

8) As you see it, what should be the function of the conscience in the maturing person?

Films described in this section can be ordered from your denominational film source or from:

Mass Media Ministries
2116 North Charles Street
Baltimore, Maryland 21218

If you do not have a Mass Media catalogue, you might be interested in ordering one for fuller descriptions of these films and others.

Notes

Few of the exercises included in the session plans could be considered original creations. Most of these structures for experience were formed by combining a variety of ideas from a variety of sources: personal experiences and ideas, experiences and ideas passed on by others, mimeographed papers, and a few books. Wherever material has been taken directly from a known written source, credit has been given to that source. This, however, does not mean that the original source has been identified, for often it is impossible to find the original source. It has been said that the structured experiences used in human relations training are similar to folk music. This is an apt analogy, for the origins of these experiences are hard to trace. I would like to acknowledge gratitude to many unknown sources.

INTRODUCTION

1. Abraham H. Maslow, *Toward a Psychology of Being* (New York: Van Nostrand Reinhold Co., 1962), p. 164.
2. Carl R. Rogers, "Learning to Be Free," in *Conflict and Creativity*, ed. Seymour M. Farber and R. H. L. Wilson (New York: McGraw-Hill Book Co., 1963).
3. Ross Snyder, *On Becoming Human* (Nashville: Abingdon Press, 1967), p. 27.

SESSION 1

1. Adapted from *Workbook in Interpersonal and Self Growth* (Philadelphia: Youth Office, Lutheran Church in America, 1970).
2. *Ibid.*
3. *Ibid.*
4. *Ibid.*

SESSION 2

1. Adapted from *Workbook in Interpersonal and Self Growth.*

2. Quoted in Patricia K. Arlin, *People* (Chicago: Argus Communications, 1970), p. 22.
3. From *Footnotes and Headlines* by Corita Kent. Copyright 1967 Herder and Herder, Inc. Used by permission of the publisher, The Seabury Press, Inc.
4. Bernard Cooke, as quoted in Arlin, *op. cit.,* p. 23.
5. From *I'll Let You Taste My Wine If I Can Taste Yours,* edited by R. Paul Firnhaber, Perspective Series #7, copyright 1969 by the Walther League, published by Concordia Publishing House. Used by permission.
6. Adapted from Richard Reichert, *Self-Awareness Through Group Dynamics* (Dayton, Ohio: Pflaum/Standard, 1970), pp. 60–62. By permission.

SESSION 3

1. Maslow, *op. cit.,* pp. 92–93.
2. Adapted from *Workbook in Interpersonal and Self Growth.*
3. Adapted from Reichert, *op. cit.,* pp. 25–28.

SESSION 4

1. Adapted from Reichert, *op. cit.,* pp. 83–86.

SESSION 6

1. Rollo May, *Love and Will* (New York: W. W. Norton & Co., 1969), pp. 243–244.

SESSION 8

1. Adapted from *Workbook in Interpersonal and Self Growth.*
2. *Ibid.*

SESSION 9

1. Adapted from Reichert, *op. cit.,* pp. 43–45.

SESSION 11

1. Adapted from *Workbook in Interpersonal and Self Growth.*